CITY21

The Search for the Second Enlightenment

By: Phil Cousineau & Christopher Zelov

Findorn Interview by: Tony Hodgson

© 2010
ISBN#9780965030670

Companion Book to the motion picture:

CITY21

DIRECTED BY: CHRISTOPHER ZELOV & PHIL COUSINEAU

1st Edition

Published by:
The Knossus Project
1866 Leithsville Road
Hellertown, PA 18055

Graphic Design: Maggie Ruder & Tzelov
Photographs by: Cousineau & Tzelov
Copyedited by: Jen Ahistrom
Printed by: Jostens Printing

D1528742

Dedicated to the Future City emerging in the depths of human creativity
and the Gallo-Roman beauty of Laurence Chassagne.

Table of Contents

Preface

Phil Cousineau

Since the Autumn of 1999, when the filming began for City 21, the documentary film that inspired this companion book, working with Christopher Zelov and the Knossus Project has been a privilege and a joy. It has also proved to be an astonishing opportunity to learn from some of the greatest architects and designers in the world what it is that makes cities thrive. Over the course of the ten years it took to create the film, and now the book, there have been innumerable moments of inspiration. The first came during the initial filming, at the Open City in Ritoque, Chile, an experimental community founded on "poetic acts of the imagination" in the sand dunes along the Pacific coast of Chile. Five years later, we were allowed to film inside Biosphere 2, in Oracle, Arizona, the most extensive closed biosystem every created. In a single day we were able to experience five microclimates, but we were also granted a glimpse of the future for sustainable designs in entire communities. Three years ago, in 2006, we ventured into northern Italy where we filmed at Damanhur, a community unique in the world for its combination of architectural sophistication, spiritual research, arts education, and goal of complete self-sufficiency.

Curiously, though, the most auspicious moment in regards for the evolution of this book, took place in 2006, at SunRock Farm, the Zelov headquarters, in the rambling countryside outside Philadelphia. As a long-time admirer of Ian McHarg, the landscape architect, and groundbreaking author of Design with Nature, Chris was eager to share something he had recently discovered in McHarg's archives, footage from his 1960s television series, "The House We Live In." The first program we watched featured McHarg interviewing Lewis Mumford, author of the highly influential The City in Civilization. After the brief opening credits, McHarg asked a single opening question that kept Mumford talking for twenty-nine straight minutes. With less than a minute remaining in the show, McHarg had time enough to say only, "I have served best by listening well."

That moment was a revelation. The phrase blazed in my mind. Those seven words helped crystallize for me what we had been doing for years on the City 21 project, journeying with our film equipment and our curiosity about the various scenarios for the future of urban life, to Chile, Brazil, and Easter Island, and on to Greece, Italy, Iceland, Scotland, England, Notre Dame, and the American Southwest.

We covered more miles than a medieval pilgrim, but our task was more complex than gathering good coverage in exotic locations. Our real work has been, "to serve well by listening," as McHarg said. In our case that has meant listening well while interviewing many of the leading architects, designers, and futurists around the world who are helping to define, with passion and clarity, what Mumford called "the city's nature and drama."

To catch a glimpse of the nature and drama of the city, we have had to cultivate an art of listening as filmmakers, but also as concerned citizens, and also as fathers who are deeply concerned about the future of cities for our children. We had to listen, as McHarg listened to Mumford, to learn what we could about what Mumford called "the city's still unrealized potentialities," from the likes of Stewart Brand, Phil Hawes, David Mayernik, Lori McElroy, Tony Hodgson, and Falco, the founder of Damanhur. And once our interviews were "in the can," we listened again to the echo of their voices in the nearly thousand pages of transcripts that needed to be condensed, compressed, and edited into a book. The insights garnered here about the future of urban transportation, energy systems, ethics and justice, communal living, food supplies, and education are a vivid reminder of something that architect Lawrence Halprin wrote in his breakthrough book, Cities: "A city, like a forest, is a delicately balanced ecosystem, always in transition." This sense of constant change and transition can evoke either enthusiasm for positive change in our urban centers—or anxiety about the decay and disintegration that set in when poor decisions are made. What the futurist William Irwin Thompson said about individuals is appropriate for cities as well: "If you do not create your destiny, you will have your fate inflicted upon you."

After sifting through and editing with Chris the reams of transcripts from our interviews, I feel like the archaeologist Howard Carter when he finally wedged open the tomb of King Tutankhamen. Asked by his fellow explorer Lord Carnarvon if he could see anything in the flickering light, Carter said auspiciously, "Yes, wonderful things."

And wonderful is how I feel after reviewing these marvelous interviews, wonderful in the sense of feeling more optimistic, more hope, more anticipation about the future.

If it's true, as I believe it is, what H. G. Wells wrote, in 1899, that "History is a race between education and catastrophe," I hope that the reader will be inspired by the visionary contributors in this book, who have trained hard and run a valiant race, while offering us a vibrant vision for the future of our cities.

Phil Cousineau

San Francisco

*Key Concepts(see pages)

* This is by no means an exhaustive list. To discover more, see the Film and Extra-Content material. CZ

Prime example of Rennaisance City Planning in Ferrera Italy. The humanist concept of the 'Ideal City' cames alive here with the work of Biagio Rossetti and his use of the then cutting edge principles of perspective.

I am not raising a Capitol or Pyramid to the pride of man, but laying a Foundation in the human understanding for a holy temple after the model of the World.

Sir Francis Bacon

"FOR HERE WE
HAVE NO LASTING
CITY, BUT WE SEEK
THE CITY WHICH
IS TO COME."
Hebrews 13:14

9

Introduction: Christopher Zelov

St. Paul de Vence

The Kingdom of France

"The City begins only when the paths are transformed into roads."
Joseph Rykert

Towards a Spiritual Hermeneitics of the City

The City was invented around 8000 thousand years ago. Most scholars think it happened first in Jericho, with the collective act of building defensive walls. Some postulate it was in Catal Hayuk, Turkey. In any event, the Idea of humans coming together to create a 'good life' and to provide protection against marauders, seems to be an enduring thrust of existence on this Earth. It is probably our most enduring invention as species.

The movement from hunting and gathering to a settled condition in a City has teleological dimensions. Indeed, urban man is more likely to feel and act as a member of a community of shared interests. Thus the Polis emerges as a force of creating citizenship, and thus seeding the rise of civilization. In fact, the word Polis has Indo-European roots which suggests that both culture and personal cultivation (education) encompass a cyclical dimension. This understanding is incorporated in the word *encyclopaideia*, which means "in the cycle of learning."

However, it was the Artists and Architects of the Italian Renaissance that are generally credited with creating the first advanced theory of the City. This augmented view involved the construction of a City designed to fulfill a variety of social, cultural, and political functions, rather than one designed solely for trade and sheer survival.

Co-emergent with the advent of mercantilist capitalism, a new leisure class with time and money to invest in cultural pursuits developed within the Italian middle class. Wealthy families of this new class entered politics, gaining power and influence in their Cities, and in most cases prioritizing aesthetic concerns.

We can add this perspective to the Moments of Grace model developed by Cultural Historian Thomas Berry as he describes it in his opus: **The Great Work.*

Key Historic Moments of Grace include:

- **the Formation of the Sun**

- **the First Living Cell**

- **Photosynthesis**

- **Control of Fire**

- **Gardens First Cultivated**

- **Fabrication of Pottery**

- **The First Alphabet**

- **Invention of Writing**

- **Spoken Language Invented**

- **1st Cities Built**

*Berry, Thomas, The Great Work, New York, Bell Tower, 1999

Further along this line, the great historian of urban life, Lewis Mumford, explained the four major transformative functions of the City as:

1. Power into Form

2. Energy into Culture

3. Dead Matter into the Living Symbols of Art

4. Biological Reproduction into Social Creativity

Thus, the City can be seen as a place for the magnification of the life process, a magic theater where characters come and go. Ultimately, it is an act of will, both individual and collective.

Naturally, some civilizations are better at it than others. Some Cities are eternal; some die a slow death. Compare Rome to Buffalo.

Indeed, we may lose our capacity to create livable cities, as J.B.S. Haldane cautioned in 1928: "The ancestors of oysters and barnacles had heads. Snakes have lost their limbs and ostriches and penguins their power of flight. Man may just as easily lose his intelligence."

Perhaps the antidote is to become like a modern Nostradamus--which translates into the desire and act of passing on our hard won knowledge to the next generation. Rosslyn, the cathedral of codes in Scotland, was built with the same intent in mind, although it's codes are in subtle stone forms, rather than prophecy inked in a book form. This takes us back to the Greek concept of Paideia, the breeding of culture in the individual and then hopefully transmitted to the society at large.

Why are most Cities based on the Grid?

It was Hippodamus, a Greek Architect, Mathematician, and Meteologos, who is credited with inventing the grid.

The Romans used the Grid not only in their military camps, but also in new colonies, capitals of provinces and civitates, as a clear representation of the order imposed by the imperial power.

The initial inspiration came from the ancient augurs scrutinizing a flock of birds for divinatory purposes, then proceeding by hypothetically dividing up the air and land along ideal perpendicular straight lines.

Indeed, the practice of symbolic forms of settlement faded into the mists of history, along with their panoply of deep spiritual and cultural signification for the indigenous populations. Once upon a time, we learn from French Anthropologist Claude Levi Straus, there was a unity between village plan, kinship system, and world view. These stratagems were almost invariably rejected, in favor of the planned grid layout, which the Europeans had inherited from the conquering Romans.

Time-tripping to the modern city, the space of mature capitalism, we plunge into the world of the "society of the spectacle," as French theorist Guy Debord put it, a world suffering from increased homogenization and generica, which the 1960s art group the Situationists proposed replacing with the heterogeneous, the rebellious and a liberating series of units of ambiance.

Again like the Surrealists, the Situationists practiced detournment, whereby pre-existing elements were re-contextualized. This disorienting strategy included reusing phrases from unacknowledged sources, reassembling film footage, or replacing part of the city with another. The famous cry of Paris, May 1968, 'Sous les paves, la plage' springs from this perspective.

City21: Multiple Perspectives on Urban Futures:

The film City21 looks at 8 different initiatives/perspectives that are shaping the 21st Century. The list does not presume to be definitive; however it does provide a revealing glimpse into some of the key projects now swaying our world into a more expansive and creative narrative.

Some of the key Design Metaphors illuminated in City21 include:

1. Classical Form and Narrative Architecture
   with David Mayernik

2. Regenerative Design and Biospherics
   with Phil Hawes

3. The Green City/The Art of Placemaking
   with The Lighthouse Project

4. Renewable Energy
   with Dr. Adalsteinn Sigurgeirsson of Iceland

5. Creating Eco-Villages
   with the Findhorn Foundation

6. Magical Architecture
   with the Damanhur Community

7. Poetry and Architecture
   with The Open City Group

8. Enduring Time/The Long Now
   with Stewart Brand

9. Forest Eco-System Engineering
   with Paolo Lugari

10. The Art of Futurist Conversation
    with Tony Hodgson + Graham Leicester

Further Key Ideas illuminated within the film:

We must invent ways to build what we want, when we want.

Creative and soulful buildings rarely happen on bankers terms. Learn from The Open City Group who have manifested a rare avant-garde experiment in Architecture and City Making.

The City as an ongoing discourse, a shared conversation.

The Greeks knew this in their bones. Indeed urban life began in Greece as an animated conversation and soon degenerated into a crude agon. As Euripedes observed "It is a slave's lot not to speak one's thought." Further along this line, Lewis Mumford uttered: "What was left of the ancient urban drama was a mere spectacle, a showed staged before a passive audience, with professional freaks, contortionists, and dwarfs usurping the place once occupied by self-respecting citizens."

Design of micro-worlds vs public space.

This is an ongoing polemic. With the new digital tools, the intensity of the debate has been ratcheted up a notch. The key to resolving this may be in an expanded definition of Self.

From our research, the key ingredient to create a new experiment in City-Making or an Eco-Village for that matter, is to find a site with a dramatic topographical edge (EZE pictured below), preferably an eagle nest of some kind.

For instance, the film illuminates 3 examples:

- Open City... in the sand dunes on the outer lip of Chile, facing the boundless Pacific Ocean

- Findhorn... the Northern extremity of Scotland, fronting the North Sea

- Damanhur... nestled in the foothills of the Alps, in northern Italy

Among the many transformations involved, the making of the City is also a story of the primal transfiguration of the wilderness into a salubrious urbane environment, a vital circuit that enhances our ability to regenerate and celebrate life.

Ultimately, it is a vehicle for survival. After all, there is a mutual arising of the City and the Self. I bring the world into being—autopoiesis, perhaps there is autocivitas as well. However we look at it, there is an increasingly complex interdependence of humans and their environment.

Cities have Mythic Histories:

**The list of the mythic origins
of Cities include:**

- Troy
  Apollo and Poseidon

- Thebes
  Cadmus and the Alphabet

- Athens
  Athena

- Eze
  Isis

- Paris
  Homer and the Odyssey

- Rome
  Romulus and Remus

- Alexandria
  Alexander the Great

- Constantinople
  The New Rome

- Jerusalem
  The Holy City

- Santa Fe
  Holy Faith

- Damanhur
  The City of Light

- Kitez
  Russian Art City, a place of justice and prosperity

- Armenia
  City in the Sky

- Shamballa
  Tibet City

- Heliopolos
  Greek City of the Sun

- Teotihuacan
  Place where the World begins

- Philadelphia
  William Penn's City of Brotherly Love

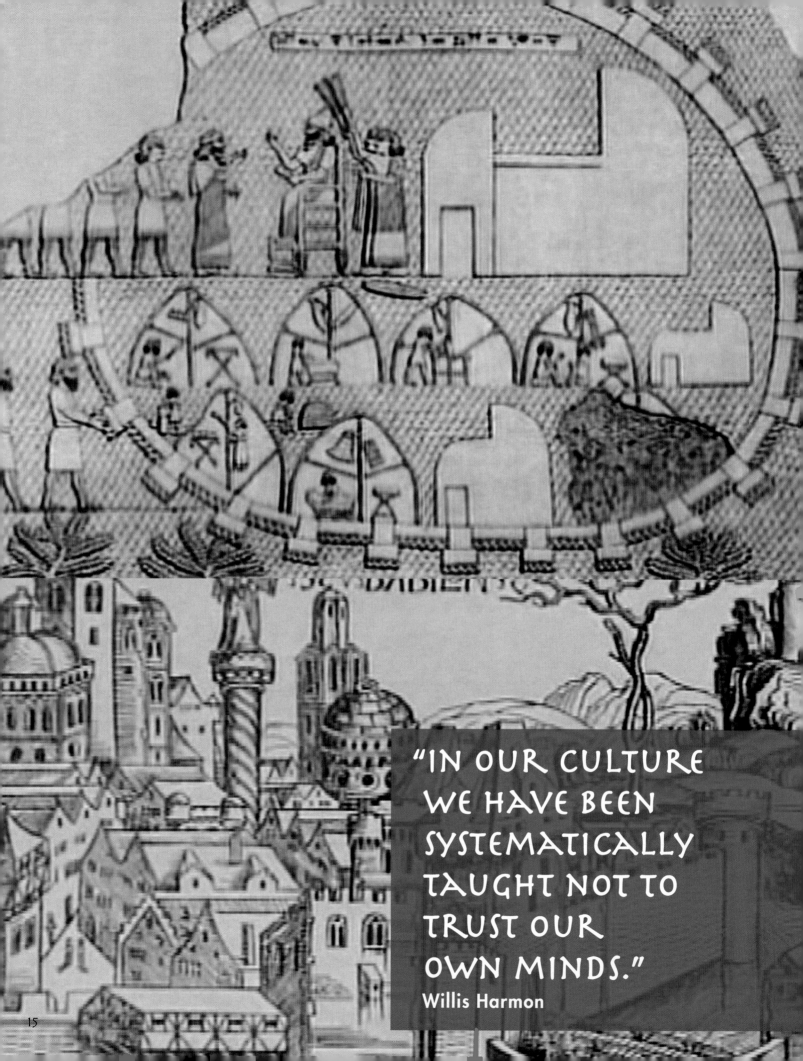

"IN OUR CULTURE WE HAVE BEEN SYSTEMATICALLY TAUGHT NOT TO TRUST OUR OWN MINDS."
Willis Harmon

According to the sages, all persons are hypnotized from infancy by the culture in which they grow up. The prime task of adult life is dehypnotization, Enlightenment—the process is discovering that the perceived world is partial and illusory, with "another reality" behind it.

Furthermore, learning to see the world with multiple perspectives is key. Swiss philosopher Jean Gebser calls it: *aperspectual space*, where one can shift around the various viewpoints in which scholars have imagined the great patterns of history playing out on the stage of time.

Friedrich Nietzsche developed a similar concept that he called: Perspectivism —which holds that knowledge is always perspectival, and there is no such thing as an immaculate perception, or epistemological absolutes. The best we can hope for is the ability to synthesize many divergent perspectives, and then arrive at a more integral way of knowing.

This is where heuristic filmmaking can intercede and play a leading role in the cultural dehypnotization process, counter-acting the claims of the dominant paradigm and penetrating into a deeper stratum of the truth.

We have unremembered many of the design lessons from medieval cities that made them such a convivial environment for human community. Indeed, the new urban response to the exigencies of the rapidly emerging Peak Oil era will involve the adaptation of new designs derived from the worlds of ecology, biology, and photovoltaics to our built environments. This will involve a myriad of new inventions, many of which were illuminated in the film: Ecological Design: Inventing the Future*.

The father of Ecological Planning, Ian McHarg, frames Paradise in terms of Agricultural values and the production of herbs and fruits---very little advanced technology in his model. His last plan the 1999 for Taiwan called: "Towards Paradise: The Millennium Plan for a Sustainable Future," is a prime example of this approach.

If we recall the classic film, Lost Horizon (1933), we will find a hidden metaphor for the lack of a positive image of the future in the popular mind. Do people even believe in Shangri La when they see it? Can it be sustained? Is it a worthy quest? Such questions linger on like a Belle Epoch Parisian lunch. Pay heed to the story of Joshua bin Joseph and how the Kingdom of Heaven surrounds us, but we do not realize it.

Historically there has been four Cultural Ecologies, according to Historian William Irwin Thompson, that have shaped Civilization since the beginning of time:

Cultural Ecology	Communication System	Polity
1. Riverine	Script	City State
2. Mediterranean	Alphabetic	Empire
3. Atlantic	Print	Industrial-Nation State
4. Biospheric	Electronic	Noetic

*see website: www.geniusloci.com

This is epochal thinking. As J.G. Bennet said in his book the Dramatic Universe: "An Epoch is characterized by a grand conception, a master Idea, which inseminated the whole life of mankind for a new harvest of temporal activities."

As Thompson further articulates: A cultural ecology is a way of knowing, an epistemology that shapes the world.*

Inherently the meme of Civilization and the meme of the City are interlinked. The Biospheric stage includes the new meme that our Cities will be based on renewable energy and contain buildings that give back to the environment more than they take. See the interview with Paolo Lugari, to discover more about this emergence.

If we can put a man on the moon, certainly we can create cities based on renewable energy. Indeed, it is a matter of social will, more than technology, which is always ready to be employed by the active imagination.

Delving into another big picture perspective, the distinguished Italian writer Giambastto Vico articulates 4 cycles of civilization:

1. Gods
2. Heroes
3. Man
4. Chaos

In terms of material usage, below is another chart eye's view:

- Age of Stone
- Age of Bronze
- Age of Steel
- Age of Oil
- Age of the Sun(renewable energy)

*Four Cultural-Ecologies, RESURGENCE (England) Nov-Dec., 1983.

As writer Joseph Rykert articulates: "the city is not really like a natural phenomenon. It is an artifact of a curious kind compounded of willed and random elements, imperfectly controlled. If it is related to physiology at all, it is more like a dream than anything else."

Furthermore, as Italo Calvino articulates it, each City presents a particular challenge to the imagination. As he writes in his classic: Invisible Cities: "Cities also believe they are the work of the mind or of chance, but neither one nor the other suffices to hold up their walls. You take delight not in a cities seven or seventy wonders, but in the answer it gives to a question of yours, or the question it asks you, forcing you to answer, like Thebes through the mouth of the Sphinx." Flashback to the enchanting archetype from the ancient world: the Temple of Apollo at Delphi, wherein the seeker went on an extended pilgrimage to the via sacra, in which a subtle narrative Architecture was employed with the intent of transforming mortal man into an immortal sage. The Great Spanish Architect Antonio Gaudi employed this theme in his acclaimed Park Guel in Barcelona where sculpture, mosaic tile, plants, and architecture illuminate the working of the symbolic alchemist's process which seeks to transform man into an immortal sage. Furthermore it is hoped that these strategic clues will help initiate the visitor into a better conceptual and artistic understanding of the site (city) and enable them to attain a higher degree of knowledge and mastery of the life process.

Might this be a desirable scenario for the Future City?

As stated in the film by Grahm Leicester: "The old rules don't seem to apply, the new rules have not been written, what we need is a Second Enlightenment."

What are some of the characteristic of the Second Enlightenment?

17

Here is a outline sketch of the elements:

- Earth Community Ethos/getting beyond the Empire mentality

- Sustainable Development/ Post-Petroleum Ethos

- Transhumanist Perspective

- Long Now Orientation

- Cross-Disciplinary Approach to Knowledge

- Dream Society, rather than just the Information Age

- Cosmogenesis orientation

- Cybernetic understanding

Clearly the eco-village movement is an indicator of this shift in consciousness about the nature and purpose of the City. As Italian writer Paolo Porttugesi articulates * **"the city represents the most extensive and violent act of man as an agent of change on the face of earth."**

Can this act be reframed into something benign and manifest the: "ability to obey the genius loci, interpreting a sort of hidden vocation of

* Portoghesi, Paolo, Architecture and Nature Milan, Skia ©2000

the landscape and at times succeeding in convincingly 'continuing' the work of creation."

The Greek drama is a study in fate, or man's conflict with the Gods. The Elizabethan drama is a study of action, or man in conflict with man. The Modern drama is a study of character, or man in conflict with himself. The drama of the 21st Century is between the Biosphere and the Technosphere, with humans playing the role of the chorus. Perhaps the same theatrical rules apply, only the stakes have risen in new degrees of magnitude.

For if Nature is reborn through the Artistic Vision, is it likewise for the City/Civilization?

Among other aspects, this film and book endeavor has been a strategic exercise in world-making. Making and remaking with all the old and new tools that are available. Indeed, we have unearthed 10 uniquely powerful perspectives/initiatives for building more vibrant and fulfilling realms in which to be human in the ever-emerging City in the 21st Century.

Dear reader may you intellectually profit from taking the time to study and learn from this voyage of discovery into re-weaving the matrix surrounding the art of City making.
Ancora Imparo.

Envisioning a Second Enlightenment
Advancing Ecology in Planning, Designing, and Building City21

William J. Cohen

Successful Cities and Urban Form

From the earliest times, when man formed human associations that would shape the first settlement patterns, the basis for the eventual form and function of the modern city was begun. Man's cities have always evolved. They have gone through many variations that reflect certain cultural needs for each successive period in history. We can study the origin of primitive villages of the aboriginal world, the formation of the monumental Greek city-states, the expansion of the cities of the Roman Empire of the ancient world, and finally the emergence of the contemporary city beginning in the medieval period to the Renaissance (roughly from 500 of the common era to the 17th century). What we will find is that all successful cities during these times shared three characteristics: they provided the rudiments of basic security for their inhabitants; they served as a center for commercial and entrepreneurial activity; and cities became a representation of the sacredness of place—especially through their religious shrines and other significant structures that perpetuated cultural myths and heritage.[1]

We will also find that cities, as they evolved, were either unplanned or planned. The *unplanned city*—oftentimes referred to as the organic or spontaneous city—could be ascribed as the dominant mode of city growth through history.

In his classic work, architect and town planner A.E.J. Morris has told us that the organic growth of cities has produced a "townscape of picturesque variety—perhaps best illustrated by medieval urban form. Despite their meandering and seemingly illogical route-structures, these town plans nevertheless clearly conform to some indefinable natural pattern." [2]

The *planned city*—also known as the created or predetermined city—became a structured, ordered, and somewhat arbitrary layout, relying on the grid and the circle as the two dominant underlying geometric forms for city development. Here a radiating street system would offer an element for connection and expansion of the basic planned form.

As history has shown, a stringent categorization of the unplanned and planned city would yield to a "blurring of the basic duality of urban form," as architectural historian, Spiro Kostof has written. He further states that "Since the early 19th century, a strand of planning that first emerges in romantic suburbs, and graduates into a full-blown alternative to the dominant practices of Western urbanism, has given us non-geometric layouts artfully designed to avoid the rigidity of geometric abstractions." [3]

However, the city is more than just a form with accompanying functions. It manifests art,

[1] Joel Kotkin, The City: A Global History (London: Weidenfeld & Nicolson, 2005), xvii-xx.
[2] A.E.J. Morris, History of Urban Form: Before the Industrial Revolutions (New York: John Wiley & Sons, 1979), 8.
[3] Spiro Kostof, The City Shaped: Urban Patterns and Meanings Through History (Boston: Bullfinch Press; Little, Brown & Company, 1991), 44.
[4] Lewis Mumford, The Culture of Cities (New York; Harcourt, Brace and Company, 1938), 3.
[5] Ibid., 5.
[6] Wilhelm Windelband, A History of Philosophy, vol. 2. Renaissance, Enlightenment, and Modern (New York: Harper Torchbooks, 1958), 447.

culture, as well as social and political values. In the view of Lewis Mumford—one of the great public intellectuals of the 20th century— "city is the form and symbol of an integrated social relationship."[4] To Mumford, "Mind takes form in the city; and in turn, urban forms condition mind….[and] with language itself, it remains man's greatest work of art." [5]

If we accept Mumford's perspective, then the true inspiration for planning and designing the city must go beyond the necessity to just provide habitat; it must represent and promote those human needs for beauty, achievement, balance, and endurance. The essential component that surfaces is that a human connection to nature becomes the inseparable bond to rivet our city-creations to our desires, our hopes, and our dreams.

For so long nature had always been there, somewhat undamaged through the building and expansion of cities. Man's tools were rudimentary, but continually advancing to allow newer innovations that would guarantee progress. Through time the increasing impact of city development on nature would march forward, ever so slowly, but more and more recognizable.

The Enlightenment and The New Progress

It was during the 16th century that a scientific revolution began, highlighted by the application of new methods of observation and experimentation to understand the laws of nature. The works of Francis Bacon, Galileo, and Rene Descartes, among others, revolutionized Western man's thinking in advancing human knowledge about our place in the world. The Enlightenment would emerge in the 17th century as the Age of Reason, promoting a rational and real world inquiry in order to apply knowledge for human benefit. Underscoring this movement—which generally would cover the period from the Glorious Revolution in England in 1688 to the defeat of post revolutionary France in 1815—was that a focus on science (conceived as the pursuit of rationality) could reveal nature as it is and show how it could be conquered or manipulated.

Of importance, it was the social and political Enlightenment philosophers, such as David Hume, John Locke, Adam Smith, Voltaire, and Jean Jacques Rousseau that vehemently rejected the religious and spiritual dogmas that had been so prominent during the Renaissance and Reformation. What they did was hold to the dictum, as stated by the English poet, Alexander Pope, that "The proper study of mankind is man." Consequently, it was this perspective that became "characteristic of the whole philosophy of the Enlightenment, not only in the practical sense…but also in the theoretical view…[that] as a whole, aims to base all knowledge upon the actual processes of [man's] physical life." [6]

The founders of the new American republic were fully immersed in the Enlightenment. All of them, but particularly Benjamin Franklin and Thomas Jefferson, were acutely aware that by studying the past they would better understand the present. And, this would serve as the basis to optimally plan for the future. Our founders were also aware of a unique and poignant fact of history—that no culture or society was immune from decline and extinction. They had read the monumental historical work produced during the Enlightenment, Edward Gibbon's, *The Decline and Fall of the Roman Empire* (1776-1788). It was that work which brought to their attention that the Romans gave up political liberty to become masters of the world. As the Romans became overextended, through an insatiable quest to conquer new lands, their empire declined.

If it was true that the great cities and empires of the past had at some point in their evolution reached their limit and simply declined, our American founders took special effort to shape a social and political system that they believed would last through the centuries. This would become for them the crucial foundation to create the new American nation.

Although the chief intellectual thrust of the Enlightenment can be said to have reached its apex early in the 19th century, the primary focus on continually improving the human condition through a rational and scientific perspective persists to this day. Yet, the seeds had been planted, and it was now up to the successors of the Enlightenment pioneers to harvest new fruit for the betterment of mankind.

In a very practical sense we measure the improvement in the human condition as progress—progress over a previous age and a previous way of living. What would happen, as a direct influence of Enlightenment thinking, is that the rational-destiny notion of human progress would spill over into how we would plan and design the most notable of human settlements—our cities. So, it was under this guise of progress that smoothed the way for technology to accelerate its forward motion to create and invent even better places to live. The machine, in the broadest context, would become the indispensable means to help and advance the human condition, proffering new artifacts to improve life, and, of course, achieve even higher levels of progress.

The machine would become both a reality and a metaphor, since it would represent the full breadth of man's conquering of the forces of nature. Perhaps nowhere has this become more prevalent than under the rubric of economic development. And, it should not surprise us that even today little or no economic value is placed on our natural resources, when measured in strictly capitalistic economic terms of supply and demand, price and profit. Nature's bounty too often is only measured as a *commodity*, and not as a *resource*. The elementary lesson that has been so difficult to come to grips with is that the value and necessity of nature affecting our lives is an inherited trait; the pursuit of economic prosperity is an acquired trait.

Realities of Progress and the Change of Direction

Progress, as a pragmatic ramification to living a better life, continued its march forward into the 20th century. Man's achievements in science, technology and knowledge reached new heights. The voyage into cyberspace would open even newer and more exciting avenues of progress. What would become recognizable is that as each new threshold was reached the challenge was always there to push even further. There would be no ultimate threshold of achievement and success, only new plateaus to reach.

As yet another door to discovery and progress opened a definable sense of loss was beginning to unfold. Were we simply proceeding too fast? Was the machine, the invention of human genius, actually pushing us into a new reality by making us subservient to its functional role? Were we allowing—consciously or unwittingly—the overwhelming success of our progress to begin to negatively impact essential components of our humanity? Were we losing the composite of a spiritual and functional relationship between man and nature?

If we think seriously for a moment about how we have built new places to live over the last several decades some stark realities begin to be revealed. While doing so we must become critically aware of two factors: first, how we are presently planning, designing, and building our cities; and second, how we are ever expanding, independent of our cities, new settlement forms into the surrounding geography, containing all of those ancillary affectations we call suburbia, edge cities, and regional conglomerations.

In retrospect we seem to have indeed opened a different door to human advancement and progress. As a result, it is not uncommon to find many people who are genuinely concerned about the state of our environment—both built and natural. The concern centers on a realization that we are really creating more problems for ourselves which do not seem to be benefiting the human condition: the accelerating decline in environmental quality; increasing traffic congestion spurred on by the indispensability of the ubiquitous automobile; the destruction of our cultural heritage, and the simmering frustration that things are just happening too fast, are all symptomatic of many people's anxiety. This is not just an awareness of intellectuals or philosophers, it is a manifestation of our present reality affecting all of us.

When Thomas Kuhn wrote his poignant masterpiece, *The Structure of Scientific Revolutions*, he found after a close examination of the history of science, that the generally accepted models, rules, or patterns by which we do things (normal science) are constantly subject to competition and change. It is through a process of competing ideas and methods that inevitably will alter our accepted models, rules, and patterns. This results in the emergence of a new paradigm (the new normal science).

Paradigms are also representative of traditions, and traditions are difficult to alter, especially when they provide a level of comfort and satisfaction to a current generation of adherents or practitioners. Yet, when an accepted way of solving problems does not fully solve the problems it attempts to address, a "failure" takes place and opens the prospect to find a new way to solve the old problems. For Kuhn this engenders a "crisis" that paves the way for a paradigm shift: "The significance of crises is the indication they provide that an occasion for retooling has arrived." [7]

We can find a parallel perspective to the Kuhnian notion of paradigm shift in historian Arnold Toynbee's assessment of the nature and pattern of civilization growth. Toynbee wrote that "In a growing civilization a challenge meets with a successful response which proceeds to generate another and a different challenge which meets with another successful response." [8] There is no end to this process and it will continue, according to Toynbee, "until a challenge arises which the civilization in question fails to meet—a tragic event which means a cessation of growth and what we have called a breakdown. Here the correlative rhythm begins." [9]

If we stand back and think about our present civilization we can positively identify a "crisis" (in Kuhn's term) or a "breakdown" (in Toynbee's term). Today, we are facing challenges that have been stewing for several decades. It is manifest in our cities—through the replacement and destruction of our historic and cultural fabric; it is manifest in our suburbs and rural hinterlands, as evidenced by sprawl, traffic congestion, and diminishing natural areas; it is manifest in the

[7] Thomas S. Kuhn, The Structure of Scientific Revolutions, 2nd ed. (Chicago: The University of Chicago Press, 1970), 76.
[8] Arnold J. Toynbee, A Study of History: Abridgement of Volumes I-VI, by D.C. Somervell (New York: Oxford University Press, 1946), 548.
[9] Ibid.

attitude and action of economic development and expansion that is threatening the intrinsic need to maintain that symbiosis between man and nature. As a result, we are now facing the reality that we have created more problems than we can solve.

The identification of the crisis—or breakdown—as it has affected the American landscape, comprising our cities, towns, and suburban areas has been going on for some time. For example, journalist James Howard Kunstler, has bluntly said, "Eighty percent of everything ever built in America has been built in the last fifty years, and most of it is depressing, brutal, ugly, unhealthy, and spiritually degrading….it is a landscape of scary places, the geography of nowhere, that has simply ceased to be a credible human habitat."[10] A less pejorative, yet pertinent analysis of the causes of the crisis has been made by architect James Wines, who recounted that "The industrial and technological influences that launched [the 20th] Century were rooted in cultural and economic change; as a result, rarely did the architects of early Modernism ever consider such issues as environmental impact, or the related psychological effects of their work on city dwellers as a consequence of this loss of contact with nature. They were committed to formalist and functionalist invention and technologies, pure and simple. [11]

Confronting the Crisis and Emergence of the Correlative Rhythm

If the crisis is recognized then it becomes necessary to prepare ourselves for a change in how we plan, design, and build our cities, including, of course, all of our future human settlements. This would be historically compatible with how Thomas Kuhn described the phasing out of the old paradigm and the phasing in of a new paradigm. This is consistent with Arnold Toynbee's analysis that after a civilization breakdown, the correlative rhythm begins.

Confronting the crisis in earnest will happen when "an individual or group first produces a synthesis able to attract most of the next generation's practitioners, the older schools gradually disappear. In part their disappearance is caused by their members' conversion to the new paradigm." [12]

The emergence of the correlative rhythm actually began long ago—in the 19th century as a reaction to the increasing industrialization that was a direct by-product of Enlightenment thinking to advance man's progress as he controlled and reshaped his natural surroundings. It began as both an artistic and literary thrust that would offer a counter position, or paradigm, to the prevailing Enlightenment influence. It would usher in environmental thinking that would exalt nature as a landscape picturesque and facilitate a transcendence above the normal and everyday acceptance of environmental destruction.

It was the Hudson River School of painting, especially the nature landscapes of Thomas Cole and Frederick Edwin Church, which brought about a popular visual awareness of the beautiful, the sublime, and the picturesque in nature. The growing American nation was

[10] James Howard Kunstler, The Geography of Nowhere: The Rise and Decline of America's Man-Made Landscape (New York: Simon & Schuster; Touchstone, 1994), 10 and 15.
[11] James Wines, Green Architecture (Köln, Germany: Taschen, 2000), 19.
[12] Kuhn, 18.
[13] Donald Worster, ed., American Environmentalism: The Formative Period, 1860-1915 (New York: John Wiley & Sons, 1973), 2.
[14] Roderick Frazier Nash, The Rights of Nature: A History of Environmental Ethics (Madison: University of Wisconsin Press, 1989), 73.

entering an age in which the fine arts helped create a new hope, and a new dream that would become embodied in planning and designing utopian communities and the early suburbs.

In 19th century America a rising cry of concern was expressed about the increasing congestion, overcrowding, and industrial ugliness of the burgeoning cities. It was a literary age and the romantic writers extolled, in both verse and prose, the wonders of nature. The rise of Transcendentalism was the literary companion to the nature landscape artists. Ralph Waldo Emerson and Henry David Thoreau led the way in writing about the glories of nature, and that without nature eternal truth could not be known. They urged a transcendence above the mundane, the ordinary, and the horrors of the industrial city. Escape to the country they invoked; there you will find peace, solitude, and God in nature.

There were a number of movements that rose and fell as a response to the environmental damage created by the industrial revolution during the 19th and well into the 20th century. These movements shared philosophical and ethical attributes that challenged the dominant Enlightenment scientific world view which generally viewed man as supreme over nature. The period between 1860 and 1915 saw the emergence of a body of thought that historian Donald Worster calls "environmentalism" which had as its central premise the view that "man's welfare depends crucially on his physical environment." [13] The contributors to this new recognition of the environment included Vermont lawyer George Perkins Marsh, landscape architect Frederick Law Olmsted, geologist Nathaniel Shaler, horticulturalist Liberty Hyde Bailey, and Harvard president Charles Eliot, among many others. What they all had in common was the raising of an environmental awareness, and the belief that planning must be undertaken to reverse the negative externalities of unchecked development in an industrial society.

After 1930 a new wave of naturalists and scientists emerged to provide further evidence and analysis as to the importance of protecting and preserving our natural resources. Their writings forged a new direction in facing the crisis of man's abuse of nature and our natural resources. Prominent among them were Paul Sears, *Deserts on the March* (1935); Fairfield Osborn, *Our Plundered Planet* (1948); Rachel Carson, *Silent Spring* (1962); Barry Commoner, *The Closing Circle: Nature, Man and Technology* (1971), and of course, Aldo Leopold, *A Sand County Almanac* (1949). It was Leopold who pushed the 20th century context of environmentalism to a new plateau when he passionately proclaimed the need for a land ethic and the view that man must become a member of the land-community, not a conqueror of it.

Leopold's contribution was especially important as has been described by historian Roderick Nash. "What he proposed would have necessitated a complete restructuring of basic American priorities and behavior. His philosophy also involved a radical redefinition of progress. The conquest and exploitation of the environment that had powered America's westward march for three centuries was to be replaced as an ideal by cooperation and coexistence." [14]

The restructuring of our present priorities and behavior has become an accelerating phenomenon in contemporary America. And, the age old Enlightenment perspective of man's achieving mastery and supremacy over nature and natural processes is becoming increasingly harmful and irrelevant. So, what do we look to in order to help us out of this senseless predicament?

The breakthrough came in 1969 with the public release of two important milestone presentations—one a film, the other a book. Both were the masterly output of the eminent landscape architect and regional planner Ian McHarg. In the film, *Multiply and Subdue the Earth*, McHarg spoke directly and passionately:

> *Show me any civilization that believes that reality exists only because man can perceive it, that the cosmos was erected to support man on its pinnacle, that man is exclusively divine, and then I will predict the nature of his cities and its landscapes, the hot dog stands, the neon shill, the ticky-tacky houses, the sterile core, the mined and ravaged countryside. This is the image of anthropocentric man. He seeks not unity with nature but conquest, yet unity he finds, when his arrogance and ignorance are stilled and he lies dead under the greensward.*[15]

The book, *Design With Nature*, would quickly become universally known as the essential direction in the planning, designing, and building the cities of today and tomorrow. It was McHarg who promoted a theory and method of *ecological planning*, predicated on the overtly simple proposition that "nature is process, that it is interacting, that it responds to laws, representing values and opportunities for human use with certain limitations and prohibitions."[16] Ecological planning by its very name establishes the linkage between man and

environment, by first understanding the values (or constraints) inherent in nature and then selecting the most suitable sites or areas to build. Through this approach we can build a hundred or a thousand new cities with the least negative impact on the resources of the natural environment. Through a concerted process of adaptation, by invoking the direction of ecological planning, we can make our lives and living conditions more in tune with our expectations and dreams for a better world.

McHarg's work has had wide acceptance, not just among planners and designers, but among a new cadre of public policy makers who recognize that the crisis is real, will not go away, and will only exacerbate if left uncorrected. Many have finally come to realize that the survival of the human species is a question that we can no longer ignore.

Envisioning a Second Enlightenment

What is now needed is a Second Enlightenment to begin to wean us from a rational-technical notion as the key framework for human progress that so gloriously characterized the first Enlightenment. The place to start down this new path is to re-conceptualize how we are living together in our cities and regions. The singular focus of this new re-conceptualization must emphasize advancing ecology in planning, designing, and building the cities of the future. The philosophical basis—in the spirit of transcendentalism—is what I would call ethical ecology. That is the conscious and deliberate way to promote an enhanced cooperation between man and nature. Moreover, it holds as

[15] Multiply and Subdue the Earth, Austin Hoyt, producer; Ian L. McHarg, organizer and on-screen host (Boston: WGBH, 1969).
   This statement appears in Ian L. McHarg, A Quest for Life: An Autobiography (New York: John Wiley & Sons, 1996), vii.
[16] Ian L. McHarg, Design With Nature (Garden City, N.Y.: The Natural History Press, 1969), 7.
   David Mayernik, Timeless Cities: An Architect's Reflections on Renaissance Italy (Boulder, Colo.: Westview Press, 2003), 5.
   I use the term, enduring to be synonymous with sustainable which has become rather overworked.
   Stewart Brand, The Clock of the Long Now: Time and Responsibility (New York: Basic Books, 1999), 118.

the highest value the interconnectedness between man and nature

The specific challenge will be to face the interplay between our aspirations and our reality, to become reacquainted with the idea of what architect and educator David Mayernik calls, "timeless cities." We need to become reconciled, once again, to the human desire for beauty in urban form, and the critical function of our natural resources to the survival of our species. We must love our cities, the old ones and the new ones that are built. After all, "The less we have loved cities, the more we have made of them what we fear or dislike; or else we resign ourselves to their aggressive banality." [17]

The human urge for exploration and discovery does not need to be squelched, but neither should it be squandered. There has always been the challenge and the anticipation to establish the ideal city. We should not abandon that urge, but look for new possibilities that are entwined within the correlative rhythm. And, it is even possible that we will discover that the ideal has already been achieved—it has been there all along, we just need to recognize it. In fact, we should turn back to history and reassess the cities of the past, carefully scrutinizing their success and become cognizant of their failures. The lessons of the past, coupled with the experiments, examples, and prototypes of today can indeed serve as guides for the future. With the current interest in building *enduring communities* and the surge in the popularity of *eco villages* there is optimism on the horizon that we are finally "getting it." [18]

If we can envision a Second Enlightenment by advancing ecology in the planning. designing, and building of City21, we can rekindle an integral substance of our humanity, by establishing a renewed connection between man and nature. We can and should plan, design, and build cities to last, not a hundred years, but a thousand years or more. Rather than planning or predicting for a single future we should reorient our thinking, as Stewart Brand tells us, to plan "for multiple possible futures, each based on a different theory of what's really going on." [19] That means that understanding the present human condition gives us the parameters to conjecture future scenarios. Part of the ecological balance in this quest is to allow the diversity of design imagination to flourish over the mundane and the boring, which is so prevalent today as illustrated by the sprawl of suburbia.

City21 becomes emblematic of a new ecological awareness in building our next cities, as well as renewing our existing ones. This awareness reinforces the age-old quest to achieve a workable and identifiable *environmental ethic*. We can begin by going beyond being philosophical. We must become committed to fuse both ethics and ecology in both theory and practice as we plan, design, and ultimately build our cities of the future. By fostering a balance between the human desire for progress and an acknowledgement of the prerogatives of nature to be of primary importance, we would advance the human condition by sanctioning a new collaboration between man and nature as the key to success and survival. This would offer a complete reversal to the conquering-of-nature approach that has been so prevalent in history. This is the essence of the paradigm shift.

The Second Enlightenment is not just a strategy. It is a call to action and a beacon to guide our planning, designing, and building. We need it to begin now. We need a Second Enlightenment to be the spark in our thoughts and actions to usher in City21 as the catalyst to re-discover our essential human aspirations and hopes for tomorrow.

CHAPTER 1

Timeless Cities

with

David Mayernik

Architect and author David Mayernik brings forth for our keen consideration a world shaped by Classical Ideals. Indeed, he uncovers an ancient language of form that once forged the lineaments of the Renaissance City and the expression of meaning in the human built world.

This quest arose out the great tradition of humanism, where there was as Mayernik articulates, **"a common mythic-narrative repertoire that could sustain a rich and accessible allegorical tradition."**

For instance, design themes in this conceptual territory include: **Hercules at the Crossroads, a Bridge as a Metaphor for the nexus between Earth and Heaven, the Golden Fountain of Friendship, the City of Light, the Golden Gate, the Champs Elysees, and the Via Sacra.**

His 2003 book, Timeless Cities, is a riveting illumination of the deeper narratives that weaved the Renaissance urban circuit with memory theaters designed to provide storage spaces for the profusion of concepts that constitute the keys to human knowledge and wisdom.

As he writes:

Cities to the European Imagination before the enlightenment were more than simply places, they were built ideas suffused with cultural memory. For a culture that had developed an elaborate visual mnemonic technique... constructed around using mental images of places to remember abstract ideas.

Furthermore: an urban landscape came to be seen as a kind of map of the mind, a three dimensional model of the mental matrix, a mnemonic mirage. For City builders for more than a thousand years after St. Augustine, the urban realm became a great memory theater where our best aspirations were played out. The place where we said the most substantial things about who we are and what we long for. The City at it's best was nothing other than a microcosm of the world, a model of the human mind, an image of heaven.

This mirror, or Parallel City, is of course spiritual yearning, perhaps a mirage, but a worthy quest to lift our minds to a higher plane beyond the cavity of rational materialism.

Instead, if we neglect our spiritual needs, we get a mundane City, as has been, according to Mayernik, the result of most City planning carried out post 18th Century. Such Cities built mainly by systems of techniques, an engineering model that seeks to program people and functions in the most efficient manner. We end up with form without meaning. The Art spirit melts away, and the values of the machine triumph.

The Timeless City approach involves:

- Sculptures that embody Ideas

- Memory Theaters that are infused with cultural knowledge

- Allegorical Architecture that speaks towards larger aspirations

- A distilled World, so we can see the fundamentals of life

To further illuminate this crucial distinction, Henry Corbin, the eminent scholar of symbolism states:

"We are no longer participants in a traditional culture; we live in a scientific civilization that is extending its control, it is said, even to images. It is commonplace today to speak of a "civilization of the image" (thinking of our magazines, cinema, and television). But one wonders whether, like all commonplace, this does not conceal a radical misunderstanding, a complete error. For instead of the image being elevated to the level of a world that would be proper to it, instead of it appearing invested with a symbolic function, leading to an internal sense, there is above all a reduction of the image to the level of sensory perception pure and simple, and thus a definitive degradation of the image. Should it not be said, therefore, that the more successful this reduction is, the more the sense of the imaginal is lost, and the more we are condemned to producing only the imaginary."

In other words, have we lost our ability to imbue our world with symbolic content beyond the quasi-imaginary discourse of politics and economics?

Can we bring this grand Humanistic sensitivity back to our 21st Century City building efforts?

Can we make the new language of Ecological Design compelling enough that people want to see it in their everyday experience of movement and form?

Is it possible, as Lorenzo Bernini desired, to make our urban theaters, "a place where our spiritual journey is ultimately played out, where in the city itself we might even glimpse some kind of spiritual fulfillment?"

Perhaps the most apropos analogy is the larva becoming an insect. When the caterpillar nears the time of metamorphosis, particular cells within the caterpillar's body begin to develop what biologists call: **imaginal cells**. Indeed, these cells start the process of creating the various parts of the new organism, the butterfly. As new parts grow and emerge, the tissue in between dissolves, and in an act of exquisite blossoming , the caterpillar becomes a butterfly.

With the advent of the complex non-linear dynamics of climate change, we have a confluence of need and procurability. Indeed, a host of new technologies are waiting to be cast, and spawn us into renewed butterflies.

CZ

Chapter 1: David Mayernik

Phil Cousineau: For the last year, those of us on the film team have been reading your book: Timeless Cities. We carried it with us to Italy when we were filming there last year. It gave us a wonderful sense of timelessness as we visited some of the cities you write about. Let's begin there: when did human beings first start making plans for the ideal city? When did human beings first think about the city as Paradise?

David Mayernik: The history I know best is actually the history of the Rome tradition. How the Italians formulated their conception of an ideal city, really goes back beyond that to Greece, to Troy. In many ways the idea of Rome is actually the refounding of Troy. Rome itself, which became such a great metaphor in the Middle Ages and the Renaissance for Ideal cities, itself is actually based on another city. Rome is a mythical refounding of the city of Troy. What I find fascinating is that all cities seem to have a mythical origin that is often another city. That is often some other foundation that they're recalling or aspiring to. So many great cities of the past aspire to other places. In many ways Alexandria, Egypt was meant to be a more perfect Athens. So all cities really hearken back to some mythical foundation. It's hard to know where that actually begins.

Cousineau: What function does the notion of an ideal city play? Is it something for human beings to aspire to?

Mayernik: To aspire to, is for me, the best way to say it. In fact, one of the things I think we've really lost is the ability to think of our cities as aspirational, as actually aspiring to something more than just document who we are and providing a context for us to live our daily lives. Cities as aspirations have something to aim for beyond contingent reality. Beyond the world we live in, the mundane, things that we go through in daily lives. In this way they become metaphors for Paradise. They become models of a kind of ideal mind that might order and structure the Cosmos. At that level they become something that even transcends earthly reality. They're more than just great cities of the past, they can even become models of Heaven, for example as they were for St. Augustine.

" THE CITY IS ETERNAL....
THENCE WE RECIEVE THE
PLEDGE OF FAITH WHILST
ON OUR PILGRIMAGE WE
SIGH FOR ITS BEAUTY."

St. Augustine,
The City of God

Cousineau: What's the difference then between the City as Paradise, the Arab idea of paradaiza, the walled in garden and Augustine's idea of the "the city of god?"

Mayernik: The difference between the idea of the ideal city as a walled paradise, an actual physical reality, and Augustine's idea of the city as the City of God, is that Augustine, ultimately, was not talking about a City that we can actually inhabit in the physical sense. He was talking about a kind of a mirror, a kind of a parallel City that exists simultaneously with the city we inhabit on earth, and it was meant to be the ideal City. The City of Heaven. The New Jerusalem. The interesting thing is that Augustine is talking about this essentially after the city of Rome has been sacked, fallen to barbarians.

Essentially, Rome, the great City that was the focus and the entity that gave idea and structure to the whole Mediterranean culture of the Roman Empire, was beginning to come apart at the seams. It was no longer really a physical center of power. Augustine rehabilitates the city by pitching it higher, by pitching it up to heaven. He provides a kind of parallel ideal City that can function as some kind of aspiration beyond the reality of cities that were beginning to come under attack and actually dissolve.

Cousineau: What can you tell a young architecture student or even a board of supervisors that the fact we're not currently living in paradisical times is not an excuse to not try to make one? Look what Augustine envisioned in a time when Rome was in decay.

Mayernik: Exactly. There's been a kind of an apology for some of the angst and chaos that we generate in contemporary culture as being reflective of who we really are, as being honest about ourselves. The reality is if that was always true in history, we would never have the great cities that we know today. In fact, most cities were built in times of incredible turmoil. Often, what the city provided was a kind of a paradise, a kind of an alternative to that turmoil. Through most of history, cities were built towards aspirations, not towards contingent reality. In fact, much of the Renaissance actually happened at a time of tremendous upheaval. Cities were always under attack. Plagues were happening. Tremendous personal and societal upheaval was happening, at the same time people are continuing building towards this more perfect vision of how society could really be.

Cousineau: What's your understanding of how the Italian thinkers made that leap of faith, between Augustine, the so called Dark Ages and the celestial vision? What do you think sparked the Renaissance? How did this notion of humanism and the designing of Cities occur?

Mayernik: I think there are a couple of different kinds of Humanisms. When this actually occurred, or how it occurred, or what was the spark of the Genesis moment. I don't know. I think sometimes we look for those things as being a kind of a big bang, as a kind of a moment of revelation. In fact, it happened progressively and in many ways it never went away. The kind of Renaissance that resulted in the Italian city actually begins in the Middle Ages when Italy was a place of urban culture while much of the rest of Europe was actually feudal. The great Italian Cities in many ways had their revivals in the 12th and 13th centuries. At that time, Sienna and Florence were erecting great monuments and building great Cities, and establishing great civic centers, all well before the Renaissance actually happens.

So the Renaissance is a kind of an intellectual idea that predates much of the most famous Art and Architecture that we associate with places like Florence. So the Florentines are talking about the Ideal City, about the idea of a Renaissance, a rebirth, the recovery of antiquity before it really even happens. They're talking about it as an Idea. In many ways, it's a literary phenomenon before it's a physical phenomenon. In that sense the idea is happening in a way before the reality can ever catch up. The Italians were dreaming of it, they were talking about it, they were writing about it before they ever really started building it.

Cousineau: Is that an illustration of the value of a cultural conversation, what you call the "communal conversation?" Can you talk about the communal dream as it is manifested in the real world, in the architecture of our cities?

Mayernik: Someone has to have the courage to draw about it, to think about it, to write about it, to dream about it. The dream has to predate the realization inevitably. That courage to dream sounds impractical; it sounds like you're not in touch with reality, you're not interested in solving real problems. But our real problems are all rooted in that lack of a dream, lack of an aspiration; otherwise we are just sort of satisfying shelter. We are just providing a kind of a physical context for our lives. We are not really providing a place that can inspire us, that can pull us out of our contingent reality and provide us an image of something better. So you have to dream first, ultimately, or else you'll never really actually achieve anything close to the dream.

Cousineau: In 1993, our Knossus Project film team interviewed Jaime Lerner, the mayor-architect of Curitiba, Brazil, for the documentary film that became Ecological Design. One phrase he

used was 'the courage to create a collective dream.' He said that we don't have the right to postpone it. Is it possible that our myth of the individual comes bang up against this mythos of the collective dream? Design for yourself and your own success versus the humanist notion of thinking about the collective. How do you feel about this collision between the individual and the collective?

Mayernik: The collective notion of "the beautiful, the new and the creative" and even "the individual and the collective" have a lot in common. They share a few things I think we've really lost in the modern world: the sense that the answers to our problems can actually exist in the past, that people might have gotten it right before us. The idea that there's somehow a city out there that's never been seen before, the City that we aspire to, but has never has been built. This tendency is, in a way, not a constructive dream, because its one that doesn't root us in our culture and in the good things that people have already done that we can build upon. The idea of standing on the shoulders of giants, is a great metaphor for the creative or inventive process, because in many ways to be really exceptional is to build on what other people have done and to take it to another level.

What we've lost is the sense that our cities can actually learn something from the great Cities of the past. Just as we've lost as individuals, as artists, as architects, the sense that we can actually build on what other people have done before us. I think we've also lost that sense as a society, and that's been true for cities in the past. They thought that their goals or their aspirations in part existed in the great Cities that predated them and then they were going to try to emulate those and exceed them.

Cousineau: Do you make a distinction between the utopian vision and the ideal vision?

Mayernik: Oh, I absolutely would, because utopia is essentially no place. That's what Thomas More essentially meant by it when he coined the word. His utopia was, in a way, a parody of the idea of the impossible city. If you root your ideas in the great things that have been done before us, you're rooting your ideas in places that actually exist, that people in fact live in. For example, we can talk about Florence as an ideal, but it's also a place that people today live very happy lives. We can learn not only from the idea of Florence as some sort of mythical aspiration, but also a day-to-day working city that functions, that has an economy, that has people that are living quite happily. Not just Florence, but Paris and Sienna, and lots of wonderful cities that are both ideals and very real at the same time.

Cousineau: As a teacher, how do you help students who want to make a mark in the world find some kind of balance between this respect for the past--and the

desire to make something new and exhilarating?

Mayernik: At that level, we have an enormous job here to do at Notre Dame in recasting their cultural conception of what it means to be creative. What it means to be inventive. In fact, the Renaissance notion of creativity wouldn't even have occurred to them. To be "creative" for someone during the Renaissance would have meant "to make something out of nothing." Only God can do that. The Renaissance culture that produced all these great artists that we know, like Michelangelo, Leonardo Da Vinci, and Raphael, would have described that process as "invention." Invention has illusions to discovery that suggest digging, finding things. Ideas are actually out there and it's our job to discover them, not to create them.

To actually create that culture here at Notre Dame is to show how one can actually achieve something by continuing to build on what skills can actually be measured and taught. To actually create that culture in a school doesn't mean you teach that creativity is something out there, that we can't possibly instruct you in, but that actually you can learn to be inventive by building on what other people have done, acquiring skills, and then saying something new with that language. What we are teaching is about acquiring skills that are analogous to learning to write, learning to speak well. Essentially, it's the same thing in the visual world, you're learning the rudiments of the language, the grammar, the syntax. With that you can say new things just as easily as you can say them in English. You don't have to reinvent the English language to say something new.

Cousineau: Can you give us an example from an Architect who has actually walked that line of honoring the past, using that wisdom but also bringing a modern flavor or accent to it?

Mayernik: The reality is we all do it. The hardest thing in the world is to so suppress your personality that there's no evidence of you in something that's actually based on the past. Inevitably, you bring something of your own perspective, your own experience, your own history, your own taste to whatever it is you create. There's some of you in everything, even when you try to exhume yourself into a tradition. In fact, it's almost inevitable that you'll provide your own spin on something you're involved with.

I think one of the great examples, and the reason why I put it on the cover of my book, is Donato Bramante's (1444-1514) design for St. Peter's Basilica in Rome. Bramante, you have to imagine, is an architect in what we would describe as almost late career. He was a man about 50 years old who comes to Rome to ostensibly study ancient Rome and to learn from the past. He wants to take a crash course in reviving the classical tradition. He's been working in that tradition his whole career. He was trained as a classical painter, but he never felt like his work was aspiring to be as good as the great examples of the past. For him, the only way to do that would be to go to Rome to measure the exemplars. He arrives at a crucial moment when the papacy is thinking about rebuilding St. Peters. Ultimately, he presents himself as being the most capable candidate to do that job. What fascinates me is the way he first described what he is going to actually do. He planned to take the two greatest buildings of antiquity and put one on top of the other. That's what the painting that I use on the cover of my book: Timeless Cities, actually represents.

Not only does he do that, before he begins his designs for St. Peters, he's given a commission to do a building on the Janiculum hill, above the city of Rome, where some people believe St. Peter had been crucified. He's going to mark this significant spot, up on the hill, with it's jagged view of the city of Rome. What he actually created was a model of a perfect ancient Roman temple as a marker for the site of St. Peters crucifixion. It's an invention of his, but it's rooted in what he thinks the best buildings of antiquity are like. It's a small building, an intimate design. It's almost the scale of a model. When you visit the Tempieto, you feel like you can hold it in your hands. Bramante makes this building, it's his own design, but it's rooted in the best examples of that tradition. Not coincidentally, he made the diameter of the Tempieto exactly the same size as the diameter of the building he was going to put on top in that composition from the past.

The Pantheon has a hole in the ceiling called an oculus. The diameter of the oculus in the Pantheon is exactly the same size as the diameter of the Tempieto. So you could imagine Bramante thinking what he's going to do is put his Tempieto on top of the Pantheon; then he's going to put the Pantheon on top of the great Basilica that survives from antiquity, the Basilica of Maxentius, which Constantine thought of as the temple of peace.

I think that by placing his own little contribution as a kind of a pinnacle on top of this assemblage of the great buildings from the past, Bramante thought he would exceed antiquity. He would build on what the "giants" before him had done. He planned to do them one better by assembling these great pieces, making his own little contribution, since the sum of those things is greater than the sum of the parts.

For me, this is the perfect metaphor of working with the past. You're both assembling and cobbling together something from past experience, but also making your own contribution. In the course of doing that, you are also possibly going beyond them, not simply imitating them. Not simply saying the best we can do is copy them. We can actually do them one better. We can actually take what they've done, understand it synthetically, holistically, and create something that transcends it. That for me is the greatest metaphor of the creative engagement with the past.

Cousineau: Can you give us a notion of the origins of the Memory Theatre, how it functioned, maybe an example or two? For instance, Cicero was believed to have been able to memorize four-hour long speeches.

Mayernik: Sure, exactly, and that's a tradition. In fact, the origins of this idea, of a classical memory technique, the mnemotechnique as Francis Yates (author of the Art of Memory) calls it, actually goes back to Greece. It's really Cicero who codifies it for the Renaissance and the Middle Ages essentially by writing it down and having it be available and accessible to them. It goes through transformations. Cicero essentially distills this idea that you can remember abstract ideas, concepts, speeches, poetry, text, by associating the ideas or even the words with images. He believed that our visual memory faculty was our strongest memory faculty, stronger than the olfactory sense, stronger than any other memory sense. Our visual memory sense was the strongest and so you could use the stronger sense to aid the weaker one. So you associate ideas with images. Now, I believe that they were thinking things worked the other way: real images, real places, cities, courtyards, sculptures, could also therefore embody ideas. It was a very reciprocal relationship between ideas and images, and they were very intimately linked. The idea that you can use images to remember text suggests that you could actually create a space that becomes a text itself. That the world could be read at some level. That you could read a Palazzo. That you could read a city as an elaborate text. The art of memory was a technique that functioned practically for them.

Ancient orators were apparently capable of incredible feats of memory. For Giulio Camillo, a rather eccentric character from the 16th century, decided that he could actually combine that system and that technique with a specific kind of visual metaphor: The Idea of the Theatre. He taught that you are more than a spectator looking a performance, or some sort of textural idea on the stage; you're the actor on the stage, and in fact the coveya, the auditorium, is filled with Ideas. It is actually filled with drawers that represent or actually contain text and that you as the actor on the stage can call forth those ideas from the drawers in

the seating area in the auditorium of this theatre. And have access to the sum of all human knowledge. It's all there, all reachable. Physically you can reach out and get it. The idea ultimately is that you're supposed to carry around that Memory Theatre around in your head. That you can actually build this memory theatre for yourself in your mind. All those ideas and all those texts are available to you intellectually and you carry them with you at some level. What it did was it also enriched the idea of what the theatre could actually be. The

theatre could become this great summation of all our experience, all of our knowledge, and all our memory. Therefore, theatre is more than just a place of entertainment. It's a place of intellectual curiosity and satisfaction. A place that we go to be enriched, to be inspired, to be elevated at some level by the experience.

Cousineau: Do you subscribe to the theory that the Globe Theatre in London was a memory theatre as well?

Mayernik: I do, to the extent that the metaphor of the theatre is a kind of summation of all our experience. There's a very common topos or theme called the theatro mundi; "The Theatre of the World." So the world is a theatre at some level. If the world's a stage, as Shakespeare says, a place where we

play out our lives, at the same time the theatre is a miniature world. The fact that the Globe Theatre is called the Globe does suggest that it's a world in miniature. It has the heavens painted over the stage to suggest that it's actually the cosmos, not just the globe of the world, of the earth, but the globe of the universe.

Cousineau: How can modern architecture use this insight to read what used to be called the libra mundi, "the Book of the World." By putting in a fountain that has some universal value to it? A cenotaph? A monument? Is this a useful notion for modern architects?

Mayernik: Absolutely. Thinking that a place should be memorable is the first step to actually making it so. You actually have to believe this stuff matters at some level. So it's not just a trope, not just a kind of a clever convention or conceit. It does say something about how our brains work. I do think that at some level Camillo tapped into something about how we actually understand things. We do understand ideas in terms of association. How we make connections between things is how we understand things. It's also ultimately how we're inventive or creative. We come up with new ideas by understanding connections to disparate ideas, things that we actually put together, is in a way, the essence of the inventive process. Thinking that the world could therefore be memorable means you have to give it structure. A chaotic place is not a memorable place. The memorable place is a place like a Theatre. One of the reasons that the Theatre could be thought of as a kind of a world in miniature is that it's a coherent world; it's a world that's more perfect than the real world. It has less of the idiosyncrasies and the chaos of the real world, but at the same time it condenses and distills the world into something essential and something fundamental that we can remember and take away. The idea that the world could also be that organized and coherent and therefore memorable is a natural extension of the idea of the 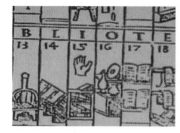 Theatre. It does say something, I think, fundamental about how we actually think and understand things; it's not just an arcane idea from the past. I think it gets to the root of how we perceive and understand things.

Cousineau: Is this how you explain Rome when you take students around? Do you try to read the city?

David Mayernik: I do. I think it's essential. In fact, Rome can't be made sense of in any other way. You can't create a map of Rome easily; the geometry of the city is very complicated. In fact, the way that you actually understand Rome is episodically. You actually are trying to put together in your mind as you experience it as some kind of complete picture, some way of understanding it as a narrative text. The Popes, in fact, did this.

Taking Posession of the City

To me, one of the great ways of explaining Rome is taking people through a kind of cross section of the city, that was this processional route called the 'Possesso Route' which refers to the "taking possession" of the city of Rome. The popes did this annually by making a walk from St. Peters to St. John Lateran on the other side of city. They picked a specific route through the city and at significant moments stopped and made reference to significant landmarks or sculptures. The popes actually began to string the city of Rome together into a kind of a story. They meant the city of Rome to be read in a particular way. They wanted it to be understood as saying something about them, as a particular pope, about the history of the Papacy, and about the very history of the city of Rome itself.

If you teach with this recognition of history, you can then also string the city together for students. You begin to see it as being stitched together as a kind of a thread of a narrative. That's only one thread. There are other threads you can take through the city. You begin to see Rome as a complex matrix of stories, that people have told for centuries, and which you can actually read as an elaborate text. People did things with this in specific ways. Architects like did like Michelangelo and the Campidoglio, for example.

Cousineau: Is anybody doing that today? Is it possible to construct a city as a narrative today? You've probably heard that the Chinese are planning dozens of these cities for the next hundred years. Do you have to start from scratch like the Chinese or can we redesign some cities in some ways to have this emotional impact?

Mayernik: The great metaphor for Rome is not some overarching kind of imposition of a logic or narrative onto the city. They did it by stitching things together, by consciously making one building reference another, consciously creating ceremonial spaces throughout the city that are ephemeral things, that are not constructions, but are actually kind of events using the city as a stage for events can also sort of reinforce for the mind of a culture, the way in which you expect it to be read. Then, how you actually make specific impositions into the city, where you put a sculpture? How one building's façade references another building's façade across town? How one building might represent the most ancient building in the city and how it draws on it and transforms it. These are conscious ways in which we can actually stitch the City together. It doesn't take a great sort of authoritarian imposition of a logic onto a city, but it takes a cultural will to do this. It takes individuals doing this in incremental ways and ultimately in the end it takes a belief in the idea that the city can be stitched together at some level.

Cousineau: I am glad to hear you have optimism about the future. Do you get it from students who are eager to hear these ideas? Do you get it from your own practice as an architect and painter? What feeds you?

Mayernik: I think optimism has to be endemic to the architectural condition. To build is ultimately an optimistic act. To really build well, though, is truly optimistic. I'm not sure that we do that very often. So I don't find my optimism comes from what we are doing today, but from what we are capable of. We have a tremendous amount of knowledge accessible to us. In many ways, we have much more knowledge available to us than the people in the Renaissance did. Our potential is greater. We have greater technology. We have tools to do things that were much harder to do in the past. One of the paradoxes of our time is that with all these incredible resources, with all this knowledge, with all this ability, that we put it to use in such trivial ends. We don't think about doing things more substantially, more meaningfully, more permanently. I think that's the great tragedy of our

time: we are frittering away these opportunities. I'm optimistic because I know it's been done in the past and with less resources. Therefore, it should be even more possible for us today. The fact that we don't do it is a wasted chance. It doesn't say that we are not capable of it. It just means that we lack the will essentially.

Cousineau: Why are we cynical about transforming the world?

Mayernik: Maybe because we have forgotten. Maybe because the dreams that the modernists had in the beginning of the 20th century proved to be failures. The dreams of the modern city were ultimately not fruitful. That idea of a City might have sounded exciting and wonderful as an alternative to what Cities unfortunately became in the 19th century, when they became places of crime and real poverty and suffering. The fact that we associated Cities with that suffering inspired modernist architects to think of a new kind of City, a City that had never existed before. As we embraced that idea and started building it, we realized that it

> " THE ROLE OF LIFE
> IS TO INSERT SOME
> INDETERMINACY
> INTO MATTER."
> Henry Bergson

had its own faults and problems and in many ways even created a worse environment. I think what we have to do is recover the ways that we used to know how to build Cities, use them to solve modern problems and solve the conditions for who we are in today and how we function as a society today. It's been done and people live in those great old Cities. It's not as if they have been abandoned. Rome is a wonderful place to live and I've been lucky enough to live there. I've lived in Florence. These are wonderful places to wake up every morning. The people who live there know that and what we have to do is recover the way to build those cities and solve the problems that we have today. I know it's possible.

Christopher Zelov: I am particularly fascinated about is the polarity between our fascination with history and our fascination with the future. Can you contrast the humanist tradition with the futurist movement?

Mayernik: I think the essence of the difference between the futurist tradition and the humanist tradition is that the futurist tradition was essentially unmoored from the past, in fact quite radically. They were not only interested in creating things that had no reference to the past, but they were often interested in quite literally destroying the past. Physically freeing ourselves from the past was supposed to liberate us to a kind of a new potential that would allow us to create things that had never been seen before.

Both the humanists and futurists are optimistic. The humanists are optimistic because of what they know we have done that is good, and so they embrace those things. They only see them as points of departure, not something that mars us in an inevitable kind of

repetition of the past. The past simply provides raw material. It provides us the skills, the knowledge, the intellectual capacity to do new things, it doesn't damn us to being rooted into a never ending cycle of repetition. It was always part of a living continuous expansive tradition.

The futurist tradition I think inevitably was reacting against something. Most movements are reactions against something. The futurists weren't reacting against the humanist tradition, unfortunately the humanist tradition was more or less dead and morbid by the time the futurists came along. What they were reacting to was unfortunately the tail end of what the classical humanist tradition became, which was the academic tradition of the 19th century, which was about repetition. Many artists and architects who were imbued with the classical tradition of the 19th century felt that the best we could do was simply copy the past, to come close to what people had done before, but never exceed it, never live up to it. Inevitably I think I would react against that if I were living in the early 20th century. I'd probably be a futurist because I would find that academic tradition deadly or be something that would sort of damned you to a never ending cycle of repeating or never even being able to repeat the best of the past. The humanist tradition is fundamentally optimistic because it believes in building on, and yet exceeding the past. The futurist movement never would have happened if the humanist tradition was still alive. Unfortunately it had been dead for 150 years.

Cousineau: What are your thoughts about what is now being called ephemeral cities?

Mayernik: This movement is based on the idea that somehow the inhabitants are ephemeral. I think then we have to make distinctions there. I think sometimes we talk about cities and we're all talking about different things. The idea that the city is ephemeral is kind of a fiction because even if cities are built poorly, they're still around for a long time. A poorly built building might last 40 years. That's hardly ephemeral. Ephemeral means things that are thrown away, transient things that come and go within the span of hours days, and weeks; maybe a year, but not over the span of decades. Decades are, at the same time, not centuries and it's not the same things as permanence. So when we talk about an ephemeral city you might think of something as a tent city, something that actually sets up somewhere and then is dismantled and moves on.

What these commentators seem to be talking about is an "ephemeral population." In that sense, the life of a city can sort of come and go in many cases cities have experienced lots of different cultures and cultures have transitioned over time. The way the people live in Rome today is not like the way they lived in it in Fellini's day. Nor is it like how they lived in it in the 19th century or the 16th century. So populations come and go. I'm an architect and I think of buildings; I think of buildings as things that stay there. Now if we mean that they were supposed to stay there, then they need to stay there for a very long time, for centuries hopefully. A building that only lasts for decades is actually a form of throw away City, which is not exactly ephemeral, but neither is it permanent and sustainable. It's not a sustainable culture. It's a throw away culture, a disposable culture. I think it neither has the poetry of what ephemeral suggests, something very lively and transient and moving, nor is it really permanent and rooted and timeless.

Cousineau: What does it mean to an architect to encounter a Timeless City? What does it mean to your own ego as an architect to possibly design something that might last for the ages?

Mayernik: I think it takes a tremendous amount of confidence, because to think in those terms, well it gives you trepidation. First of all, you have to be sure that what you're doing is actually something you want to be around for more than a lifetime. One of the reasons we have a throwaway culture is that we're not really committed to any real ideas. One of the reasons we feel that we can recycle or rehabilitate our buildings, replacing them with new ones, is because we think that ideas might change in 40 years. To talk about timeless things is to talk about the things that don't change. What appeals to anybody who is interested in history, or is interested in reading anything that's written before the last couple of decades, is the sense that the human experience hasn't, in many ways, fundamentally changed for thousands of years. The things that concerned writers like Cicero or Juvenal or Virgil or the Greek writers are the same human emotions that still come up today. The same desire they had for the "good life," is in many ways, the same desires that people still have today. How we actually define the good life in terms of the things that we have, in terms of the things that we use as products. Those things come and go.

The desire for happiness, the desire for a civil society, a just society, all those kind of things haven't fundamentally changed. Those dreams and aspirations for the things that are timeless in the human condition have got to be the things that inform what we do as builders of Cities, because the other stuff is going to come and go. How you define immediate, short term economic or financial success, those things are going to change over time. How we define entertainment might change over time, but the deep longings of the human condition, those things I don't believe change. The way I know that is by going to cities that were built by people who in many ways lived radically different lives than the kind of life I live today. By going to those places and feeling at home, in some cases more at home there than I ever felt in the world that I grew up in-- suggests to me that there's something there that is timeless that we can build on. In fact, they mean more for us today, than the world we're actually wind up building.

Cousineau: Pericles wrote in the 5th century that his dream was to build a city in which ordinary citizens could lead what we called "the good life." What does the good life in a good city mean to you?

Mayernik: Some of it is day-to-day reality, the thought that there's actually pleasure in waking up every morning and walking to work. The fact that you can walk to work might be an aspect of that. Some of it is just the physical aspects of it. Proximity of things, having things accessible to you; that you don't have to get in your car to do everything. There's actually really something wonderful about being able to walk out your door, finding a coffee shop, having a place to go to the post office, do your shopping and go to work and do all the things you need to do in your daily life. It's kind of mundane stuff and that's just the kind of practical satisfaction of the daily needs of your life. There's something also rewarding about the beauty that you encounter every day when you walk to work; you might see something new and surprising. Again, I've been blessed by having experiences in places like Rome, where one can do that within the span of a five minute walk, one can experience something new every time. There's a great Italian expression about Rome, 'Nome baste on vita,' "one lifetime is not enough to really see and understand Rome." This is because so many people over so many years have invested their heart and soul into building everything that they do there well, investing it with art and craft and meaning. It's not that we don't have that here in the United States.

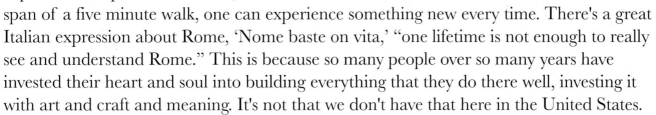

In our cities that have preserved some sense of continuity in their culture, we do have that. There are wonderful, rich experiences in New York City or Philadelphia, where my wife is from, where I met her, and where I know well. Philadelphia is a great city with history, and there is a sense that you can discover new things every day. That sense of a city as a source of pleasure. That you get enjoyment out of it. It's not trivial pleasure. It's something that touches your soul, but in order to have that each one of us has to think that everything we contribute to the city matters. It's going to matter, not just to us, but to everyone else who's going to experience it and know it. You have a collective responsibility every time you put something into a political social context, you're contributing something, not just to your own life, but to everybody's life. If we took that seriously as a culture, we're absolutely capable of making places like that again.

CHAPTER 2

Biospherics in Eco-Village Design

with

Phil Hawes

"IN EVERY REBELLION
IS TO BE FOUND THE
METAPHYSICAL
DEMAND FOR UNITY,
THE IMPOSSIBILTY OF
CAPTURING IT, AND
THE CONSTRUCTION
OF AN ALTERNATIVE
UNIVERSE."
Albert Camus

Phil Hawes has taken on the audacious and highly relevant challenge of re-designing the sprawling American settlement pattern into a Eco-Village scale and form.

Not content to join the business as usual crowd, he seeks to bring forth a new way of establishing the human presence on the land.

Engaging the Middle Ages village as a model, inspired by ancient villages in France like Eze, Lombez, and Gordes, Hawes seeks to plant a fertile seed to re-invent the ekistical reality of America in the 21st Century. An ekistical reality that in it's current form is bankrupting us, according to the writer James Kuntsler*.

We post-moderns shaped by the illusion of cheap oil in the 20th Century are like the chained prisoners in Plato's Cave, only seeing the reflection of our bias against the wall of our time. To escape this predicament and to see with a more discerning lens will require a new acquaintance with the multiple facets of Natural Law. Indeed, shifting from an Empire orientation to one of the Earth community involves a greater understanding of our place in the Universe. Read the book: The Great Turning by David Korten for more insight on this subject.

The laws of the nature understanding enshrined in the 1st paragraph of the Declaration of Independence, are part of the source code that can deliver our civilization from the petroleum imbued landscape we have fabricated and marinated overselves in over the last 100 odd years.

In sooth, building the Green Infrastructure is part of the key challenge of our time.

According to Hawes, getting into the deep mind of Biospheric Time is a clue to creating more enduring forms civilization.

Community design based on the principles of Biospherics may be how the next evolutionary stage of the American landscape is shaped. Phil Hawes certainly thinks such.

The historic polemic has always been Babylon vs Jerusalem in the building of our urban worlds. Jerusalem emerges when we build with the active imagination.

Babylon reigns forth when we build for only short-term material gain, with no reference to the needs of the human soul.

Look around you now, which do you think has dominated?

There is another way, let's open the door beyond oil with Dr. Phil Hawes..........

CZ

Themes:

- What's next after Empire?

- Eco-Villages as an alternative form

- Middle ages village as a model

- Biospheric time

- Evolution of the Biosphere 2 project?

*see: Home From Nowhere, Simon & Schuster, New York, NY 1996.

Chapter 2: Phil Hawes

"Ecovillages are a viable solution to the eradication of poverty and degradation of the environment. They combine a supportive social-cultural environment integrating spirituality, ecology and sustainable business development with a low impact life style."
John Clausen

Phil Cousineau: Every great story has a great beginning. Every innovation has a great story. We're interested in yours. Can you describe your vision for rebuilding our communities? Where did it all begin for you?

"I THINK IT IS TIME FOR BUSINESS AND ECONOMIC METAPHORS TO SHIFT FROM SPECIES-BOUND EVOLUTION AND POND/FOREST ECOLOGY TO THE MORE DYNAMIC PROCESS OF MARGULIS'S MICROBIAL SOUP, WITH FAST CYCLING (HALF-HOUR REPRODUCTION), EXPLOSIVE DIVERSITY, CONSTANT AND WANTON TRAIT EXCHANGE, AND EMBRACE ANYTHING SYMBIOTIC STRATEGIES."
Stewart Brand

Phil Hawes: That's a very interesting question. The vision for me began one night when I was drying dishes in New Mexico where I had been living for 20 years. The man who put the community together was John Allen. So I remember thinking that night, "John has a really great vision. I don't have a vision. I'm going to follow his vision until I get my own." That was the first time I thought about having a vision, a goal, an idea of what you want to do with your life. Suddenly something appears in your life that is important for you to follow. That was my first connection with the idea of having a vision. I ended up working with John and the other people in his group on the Biosphere 2 project for 20 years.

When I decided to leave the Biosphere 2 project I asked myself, "What am I going to do now? That's a hard act to follow, that Biosphere, but it's got to be leading into something. What's it leading into?" What I figured for myself was that I had learned certain things on the Biosphere project, and I learned other things by working with a group of people for 20 years. I considered the possibility of going back into the art world because at one time, I had worked with gold and silver, and worked with aluminum casting, and made sculpture, and even did a little bit of painting. But then I thought, "No, I can't do that because I've learned too much on the Biosphere project, and I've got to do something with it."

I think that the Biosphere 2 project was very, very important, I spent 8 1/2 years of my life on it. But then I realized that it was just one step and that the next step was to take what I'd learned and apply it to human communities.

My interest in neighborhood development and communities dated back to 1963 when I studied planning in graduate school. I never wanted to build skyscrapers. I've always been oriented toward small-scale communities.

Around 1991 it all started to coagulate. I started studying more and more of Ebenezer Howard and other great planners, and decided that architecture was all very well, but I'm really more interested in developing the framework to build communities. I guess you could say it took 40 years or so for me to get the picture of what was going on with my own vision, my own particular obsession. So I'm pretty obsessed with that idea of building communities that are ecologically sustainable.

Bright Lights, Big City --Or Small Lights, Small City

"No system or machinery or economic doctrine or theory stands on its own feet: it is invariably built on a metaphysical foundation, that is to say, upon man's basic outlook on life, its meaning and its purpose. I have talked about the religion of economics, the idol worship of material possessions, of consumption and the so-called standard of living, and the fateful propensity that rejoices in the fact that what were luxuries to our fathers have become necessities for us."
Ernest Schumacher, Small is Beautiful

Cousineau: Of late, there has been a great deal of discussion among architects, designers, sociologists, and futurists about what do with the accelerated growth in megacities like Mexico City, Cairo, Sao Paolo. The question is how to save them, renovate them, rehabilitate them, help them save themselves. You have said that these megacities may be beyond saving, so you're focusing on smaller communities. Can you tell us why? Why should we be thinking small, building small?

Hawes: Big cities versus small cities, or small towns, small communities. Basically, I'm a small community type of guy. I don't enjoy being in big cities. Aside from that, I'm not saying nobody should be involved in big cities, or that nobody should stop trying to change them. It's just not my particular interest. I'm just old enough to know that I don't have enough time left to get involved in existing big cities. I think it's the type of task that is a life work. If you're just emerging out of planning school, maybe you'll want to devote your life to the big cities. I feel that the good old boys system that every community has developed in the bigger cities has mostly served to stifle change. I believe that

change is completely necessary. We can't go on the way it's going on. I don't believe that cities with a population of 20 million are viable. I'm far more interested in starting from scratch. That means starting on cheap land instead of going into a situation where the land prices are sky high. If you're starting with cheap land, you can build a community that is not overpriced.

There are a lot of socioeconomic ideas that I'm interested in. For instance, how can an average person, the guy that's flipping burgers down at McDonald's, own a good home? How can this guy and his wife own not a factory built home, but one made out of real materials like mud, adobe, rammed earth, rock? Small is not just beautiful, but small is doable.

Now, I figure I've got maybe 10 more years of useful lifetime. That means I can probably accomplish something small, rather than going into New York City or Tucson and not accomplishing much. The political structure of any city is so well organized and so tight that it's very difficult to make change happen in a place like that. I'm all for radical change. I'm just not interested in a little bit of in-fill and a new pocket park over here. I want a radical change so that everybody can have a fantastically interesting, exciting life.

> " CHARACTER IS HIGHER
> THAN INTELLECT."
> Ralph Waldo Emerson

Cousineau: Recently, you spoke about the importance of principles in urban design. Could you enumerate the principles behind your teaching, your design work, the principles behind eco–village creation?

Hawes: Principles are rules, right? It started when I was teaching at The San Francisco Institute of Architecture, which is devoted to the organic school of architecture. I tried to talk with the students about what is important. To do that, I taught them about the four things that I think that are doable for the average individual to actually make a difference in his own life: 1) water, including waste water; 2) energy, including non-fossil fuel, renewable energies that you would use; 3) the food that you would grow and eat; 4) the materials that you build your houses or buildings out of. Those four things are very simple and very basic. If you can get any kind of control over your life in any of those four areas, which is possible to do, then it's possible to gain a little more control over your life. Right now almost nobody has any control over those things with respect to their own lives.

So that was my starting point. When I looked into the values by which you start to build a community, I realized that the values are where you have to begin. Then from the values, you derive your goals, and from your goals, you derive your policies that you put into the government; and from the policies, you derive the programs. You don't just go out and create programs [out of nothing]. When I came up with the program, I realized that the program was coming from my own values, my own goals and my own policies. That's the way I started.

Work Ethic

Cousineau: I've long been fascinated with the work ethic of creative people. To paraphrase Edison, how do you move from inspiration, through the perspiration, to get things accomplished in life? What is the fire that drives you, that drives the dream?

Hawes: I'm a real emotional guy. About 10 or 12 years ago, I came to a conclusion that there are only two important things in life. One was love and the other was the spiritual search. Everything else is icing on the cake. All the things we do, such as building towns, writing books, making music--all these things are great, but they're just ways of expressing deeper things that are even more important.

Cousineau: You seem to be a man who is ahead of his times, which is usually marked by resistance to ideas. How can you feel confident that after working with these designs for a couple of decades that there are kindred spirits who will want to live in your eco-villages? Where do you find the courage to move past the inevitable obstacles in your work?

Hawes: I don't really feel any resistance. Everywhere I go, it's the other way around. This is part of being obsessed and mad. I feel, I see, I find a kind of desperation in many people accepting these ideas, even if I've got only one thing I can point to that I invented completely on my own. Everything else is pretty much like the Biosphere 2 project. I find comfort in knowing my partner there John Allen said, "It's not that we're doing anything different or anything new, we're just bringing it all together in one place at one time." Now this is a critical aspect of trying to build an ecologically sustainable community. The ideas are already out there. There's almost nothing in architecture and design that hasn't already been done some place at least once. However, it's never been brought together in one place at one time and done all together. At least not until our Biosphere 2 project.

" THE ROLE OF LIFE IS TO INSERT SOME INDETERMINACY INTO MATTER."

Henry Bergson

"Eco-villages are not your parents' communes. While some can trace their roots back to the counterculture of the '60s and '70s, few today identify with the "hippie" stereotype. Members are generally hard working, environmentally and health conscious, and family oriented. Anyone who believes eco-villages are marginal or irrelevant is not aware of current global trends. Essentially, eco-villages represent humanity's best research and development laboratories for how we can learn to live well and lightly."
Daniel Greenberg, founder "Living Routes" interviewed by Tim Patterson, MatadorTrips.com

Cousineau: There is a long track record of short-lived eco-communities or failed attempts at creating a green or sustainable community. Do you recognize any long-term successes, any projects that have defied the odds?

Hawes: The closest thing that I've ever heard to a long-term success is the community in Colombia, which is called Gaviotas. That's very, very close to being a completely ecological and sustainable community. Certainly, the way they went about it is innovative. They have their own industry, and I think that's one of the main things to start with. You don't start by building the houses. You start with industry and then people that work there. The industries are those that are necessary to build a town, such as the woodworking, the foundry, the machine shops, the metalworking. For example, if you're building wind generators, cabinetwork, or furniture, you should try to promote those industries. The people who would work there and actually create the town would probably also want to live there. Fifty percent of them would, more or less. It just makes sense that you build houses for the people who are actually building the town.

Let's say we start a woodworking shop and sell it to the people that are working in the shop, and say, "Hey guys, you have approximately five years of a captive market here." If you can't develop your market to expand that beyond part of the town at the end of five years, you may be out of business. But at least you've got five years in which to develop your business and try to get more business other places.

The Power Of Mentors

"A mentor is someone whose hindsight can become your foresight."
Anonymous

Cousineau: It seems to me that everyone who is inspired has been inspired. Inspiration can come from a place or a person, or from a bolt out of the blue. Who or what has inspired you, stirred you, kept you on the path?

Hawes: Of the people that have inspired me, there are those whom I met during my experience in Mondragon, Spain, as far as cooperatives are concerned. As far as teachers go, Lewis Mumford was a huge influence in my life, as was Ebenezer Howard, the great English planner of the early 1900s. The whole thread of city planning was inspiring when I did two years of graduate work. That's when I became fairly familiar with some of the great ideas and thoughts in the history of city planning.

More than anything else, the medieval village has been my role model. The medieval village taught me that the ideal size for communal living is usually never more than 5000 people. I learned that those villages were divided into quarters, four parts. Each of these so-called quarters might contain a parish church. The main church would be in the center of town. Eventually, the Church found that about 1500 people was a pretty good administrative size. According to the research that I've done, a parish would be roughly 1500 people. If you put them all together, you'd have around 5000 or 6000 people in a town. That's the optimal figure that I've been working with in order to build the kind of ecological village that I'm interested in. This range of population will give you a full service community, enough people so you can have your own internal transportation system, like a cable car, and you can eliminate the automobile from being the main fabric of the town. It's large enough so you can have your banks, you can have your shopping. You can certainly have everything that you need so you don't have to start commuting every day to do your grocery shopping or your work for that matter. Again, the main idea is that people who live in the town can, to a great extent, work in the town.

"The value of the personal relationship to all things is that it creates intimacy...
and intimacy creates understanding... and understanding creates love."
Anais Nin (1903 - 1977)

Cousineau: Many scholars, such as Thomas Moore and novelists such as Anais Nin have written about the role of intimacy in building communities. According to your view, does it matter if we live in a smaller size village with people you actually know by their first name? Does size matter?

Hawes: The intimacy that you might experience in a small size town compared to a large town is debatable. I'm not sure that you couldn't have the same sort of intimacy in a neighborhood in a large city that you'd experience in a small town. I used to live in a small part of Indianapolis, Indiana, back during World War II. It was a very interesting community, similar to this town that I live in now, Oracle, Arizona, which is around 3500 people. I don't know that many people here, maybe a couple hundred people. I don't circulate around a whole lot, but I think it's not so much who you know, as the way the fabric of a town is integrated and the level of participation you have there, which is a different level of knowing. We have a lot of interesting characters around here, like our beekeeper who sells his honey, and is also a singer who makes and sells his own CDs. Intimacy is beyond just the face-to-face knowing people.

Biosphere 2: Total Process Design

"We have the ability to be a creative, cooperative agent with evolution. This is what I call victory."
John Allen, co-founder of Biosphere 2

Cousineau: On the other side of the spectrum of your small-scale work is your with work at Biosphere 2. You're considered the primary architect, one of the prime movers of that epic project, which is arguably one of the most significant architecture and design accomplishments of the twentieth century. What did you learn from that experience and how is it influencing you now with your desire to create eco-villages?

Hawes: What I learned from the Biosphere 2 experience is not quite that simple. I had a relationship with the people I was working with there that went back 15 years. When we started working together, we made a decision we would work only on ecological projects. It all began around 1971 when we started working together on a series of urban ecological projects, grasslands projects, mountain projects, and desert projects. One of our guiding ideas was "total process." For example, when we built the adobe houses in Santa Fe, New Mexico, I had licenses to do it all. We purchased the land, we did the master planning, installed the infrastructure ourselves with our town licenses. We built the buildings. We had our own sales department. We sold the buildings. We did our roofing. We did our electrical. We did our plumbing. We didn't have any outside contractors. At the height of that project there were 110 people working on the project. We worked a 4-hour day 4 days a week and paid $4.00 an hour. That was pretty good money in 1974, in Santa Fe, New Mexico.

Another original idea was that we would hire people who were writing novels or painting or doing something else that was creative. We hired people who had another life besides working on construction sites. They would do their own creative work in the afternoons after they'd work on construction with us in the mornings. That proved to be very interesting, and it's brought some fascinating feedback over the years. One of our more memorable workers was writing the great American novel, but instead of pursuing his book he ended up getting his plumber's license. Today he's a plumber in Tucson, Arizona. Funny things happen.

So I believe that trying to do a "total process" is very, very important. Another very important idea is to encourage your team to think in terms of enterprise-not in terms of jobs, getting jobs, providing jobs. An enterprise fits in with my ideas about how our corporation starts a wood shop. Eventually, we want to sell that wood shop. We don't want to be in the business of running wood shops; we want to be in the business of building ecological villages. The wood shop should be owned by the people who work in the wood shop. They wouldn't just have a job; they would have an enterprise. My job is to do just that: promote enterprises.

The Great Paradigm Shift

"Rather than being an interpreter, the scientist who embraces a new paradigm is like the man wearing inverting lenses."
Thomas Kuhn

Cousineau: How did we get into this paradigm?

Hawes: This paradigm began 10,000 years ago as cities developed and it became necessary to get more land, because you had a surplus. With the rise of cities, you started getting rulers, you started getting armies, and you started growing and taking your neighbors land. You also needed slaves, because you needed more people to work the land. This may be an empire paradigm that's 10,000 years old from the time we quit being hunters and gatherers. One way to get out of this is not to go back to hunting and gathering, but to go back to the village compound. But this is very tricky.

Let's say you make your town of 5000 people sustainable. The way I define sustainable is not the way everybody defines it. I think that something is sustainable if you can continue to do it for 1000 or 2000 years without destroying the environment. Otherwise, you're destroying the environment. If you can't do that, you can't sustain. By the way, when you look it up in the dictionary the word "sustain" means "to hold up or support

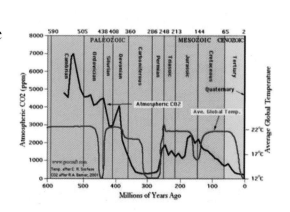

indefinitely." So if you're doing things that are sustainable with respect to your food supply it means that you are doing it in a fashion that you can continue to do for 1000 years without destroying the land and your environment. This is really difficult because we're not doing anything sustainably in the modern world. Not growing food, not making clothes, not transportation, not building houses, not providing energy for ourselves. None of this. We're not taking care of our water, not doing the proper thing with our waste water. None of these things are being done in a fashion that can be continued for 1000 or 2000 years.

"We need to shift the paradigm from reactive technologies to more integrative solutions that deal with the variety and complexity of the threats that are out there today."
John W. Thompson

Cousineau: Our dependence on foreign oil seems to impact virtually everything in the modern world. How does it influence the way we are able-or unable-to design our cities and communities?

Hawes: This is a serious problem. The whole world is floating and driven by a sea of essentially free oil and has been for the last hundred years. This dependence is the culmination of maybe 10,000 years but has seriously intensified in the last 100 or 200 years. If you develop a certain mindset, you can get out of it. One way to get out of the dependence is to completely collapse and fail, to be destroyed and implode, and endure huge die-off's of human beings. That's one way to get out of this tragic paradigm. There are a few of us who think that there may be other less dramatic ways to get out of the dependence that may not cause this kind of social upheaval, the destruction of human life, and devastation of the environment. We're at a very dicey point in history. We need

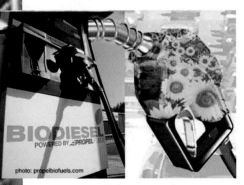
photo: propelbiofuels.com

to start doing some real serious work, and not just try to do business as usual, the same old, same old, every day. Or say: We'll just put a little more green over here, and we'll clean up our act a little bit over here. No, I think it's going to take a revolutionary approach to get us out of the old dependence paradigm and take us into a new independent one. Everywhere I look, I see people interested in doing that. Everywhere I look, I see people who know how to do that.

The Path That Is No Path

"If you follow a path in the forest, it is not your path; make your own path."

from the King Arthur legends

Cousineau: What you're describing to me sounds something like the "ancient

future," design ideas that evoke what we feel when we're in the ancient villages of Europe or Asia or Africa. Is there such a thing as a path of "timeless design" in what you are trying to bring into eco-village architecture?

Hawes: Philosophically, the idea of a path that the Native American people and other traditional peoples have is fantastic, but who among us has a path? What path do we have in terms of our background, our Scotch, Irish, Welsh, French, German, or English like myself? Unless you're part of a tribal group, you probably don't have a path. People in various religions have a bit of a path that can be followed, but it's not always a path that would be ecologically in synch. Still, I think it'd be great to have a path.

Everyone throws the word paradigm around, but I always substitute the word "worldview" for the word paradigm. If your worldview holds that the most important thing in life is getting a bigger car, or a bigger house, or more money, well, that's not a great worldview to have. It doesn't really take you anywhere except to a place where you have bigger things. I mean, how many cars can you drive? I've had this discussion with people who were talking to me about having millions and millions of dollars. That's great, millions of dollars are good, but what are you going to do with it? If you're not going to do something with it that's interesting and productive in the sense of producing a better life for the people in the world, what is it worth? Who is worth millions of dollars on their own? Who can say, "I have actually through my sweat and my effort, I have created, I have earned $10 million?" Nobody earns $10 million. It comes from other people's effort and you just happen to be clever enough to siphon it off one way or another. Nobody earns that much money on their own. How much per hour, for example, can you reasonably charge? Ten thousand dollars an hour? For what? What do you know that's worth $10,000 an hour that I don't know or somebody else doesn't know?

All these are very interesting questions. But as far as having a path goes, I don't think I really have one. If I had a path like Native American tribal people have, I would probably be in a much better position than the one I'm in. The experiences that I've had as a person, whether it's cooking, or cleaning out the bathrooms, or digging ditches in Australia, or running a ship, are all very good lessons because you're allowed in the environment. If you're lucky to do different kinds of work, you don't start thinking, "I'm up here, and those guys are down there." It's really very valuable to experience many things in life. The kinds of work that you do determine where you think you should be in this society. The closest thing I have to a path is my work.

" EVERY BLADE OF GRASS IS A JOURNEY WORK OF A STAR."
Walt Whitman

Factoring In Beauty

"Ever bigger machines, entailing ever bigger concentrations of economic power and exerting ever greater violence against the environment, do not represent progress: they are a denial of wisdom. Wisdom demands a new orientation of science and technology towards the organic, the gentle, the non-violent, the elegant and beautiful."

E.F. Schumacher, Small is Beautiful

Cousineau: Beauty has played a vital role in design and architecture as far back as we can track in history. For the Greeks, if a building or a body wasn't beautiful, it wasn't true. In our own time Bucky Fuller said he knew his work was finally right when it was beautiful. What role if, any, does beauty play in your work?

> " ART IS THE PATH OF THE CREATOR TO HIS WORK."
> Ralph Waldo Emerson

Hawes: When I think about this business about creating ecologically and economically sustainable communities (ecology and economy mean almost exactly the same thing) I think about the beauty of it. What I'm interested in doing is creating an art form out of the building eco-communities.

For example, if you have in your sustainable village industries a ceramics industry you can have your roofs covered with ceramics. Let's say that your roofs are mounted on a very thin cement, shell roof structure. The ceramics can spill down the walls of your rammed earth buildings, across the pavement of your walking streets, into the houses, up through the steps into the houses, across the floors, up onto the counters, into the bathroom, the walls, the ceilings.

That's just one possibility. Maybe not everybody's going to want to have a ceramic roof. But I think that one of the first industries that should be developed in a sustainable town is the ceramics industry. The energy involved in creating ceramics is high, but the longevity (and beauty) of that object can be impressive. Recently, I saw ceramics in Europe that were 1000 years old, and you can see ceramics in Egypt that are 3000 to 5000 years old. A lot of energy goes into that piece of clay and the glazing, but it's going to last and last and last and can be used over and over again.

To me, an important aspect of beauty, is its longevity, the ability of an object to transfer itself or live through generation after generation after generation, and be appreciated for its value, for its appearance.

Creating Continuity In A Restless World

"Those who are restless have no home; those who have no home will never rest."

Greek proverb

Cousineau: We live in an increasingly transient and restless world. Stewart Brand tells us that the average building lasts only fifty years. How can anyone create a sustainable community with such a restless population?

Hawes: Why is the population restless? Why do Americans move every two- point-whatever years? I believe in searching for something. I would imagine they're looking and they're not finding. Whatever it is they're looking for is not being found. I don't think you can pin it completely on economics. People don't just move because they want to get a different job. I think that the actual physical appearance that we look at every day, every day, every day is so bad that it drives people to want something, anything different.

Speaking personally, I might try to see something different by moving, going somewhere else. Let's say I heard that it's really beautiful in Colorado and so I go to Denver. What do I see? The same thing I saw in Ohio. Or I go from Denver to Spokane. What do I see? The same thing I saw in Albuquerque.

As far as the street scene goes, and the road rage, and the strip malls in America today, it's very difficult for architects. To create beauty in this culture is hard, because it's so hard to find beauty in this whole hideous scene. There's something like 20,000 architects a year that graduate from school in this country. How can we expect them to create beautiful projects if so few of them have ever seen anything beautiful?

" IT IS EITHER EASY OR IMPOSSIBLE."
Salvador Dali

The Future Of The Human Adventure

"Plunge boldly into the thick of life, and seize it where you will, it is always interesting."
Johann Wolfgang Goethe

Cousineau: Could you expand a little bit on something you said earlier—that you keep going with this work because you don't want to see the human adventure fail?

Hawes: It's not that I keep going because I don't want to see the human experiment to fail. It's that I think that the human experiment is extremely important. That's something that drives a lot of people, whether they really realize it consciously or not. They know that we're in really deep trouble. As a species, we're destroying ourselves and we're destroying other species. We're taking the world down with us, so to speak, if our human experiment fails.

There's a great line in Faust by Goethe where Mephistopheles, the devil:

"It would be better if creation stopped, so why don't you call ruin down, for a catastrophe scene, is what I revel in. I build millions every year and yet there's always fresh young circulating blood. It makes me mad to see from earth, and air, and water, all these seeds and germs advance through drought and flood, ice age and tropic. Fire is mine. The power of fire and nothing else to call my own."

Here's a creature that is the force that controls fire, atom bombs, a destructive force, a force that says it would be better if creation stopped. A lot of people, whether they know it or not, believe that it would be better if creation stopped. I used to tell my students that Star Wars is really true: you've got to choose sides. Are you going to be on the dark side of the force or the light side of the force, as you see it? You've got to choose the best you can. You may make a mistake, but still, you should choose. That's what I think about with respect to us not letting the human experiment fail.

"Who dares nothing, need hope for nothing."
Friedrich von Schiller

What Then Shall We Do?

Cousineau: In his spiritual memoir, Confessions, Tolstoy asks, "What then shall we do?" What do we know when we are backed into a corner, when we are afraid of the future? Regarding our perilous moment in history with our energy crisis, what then shall we do?

Hawes: The question is really about the post petroleum period. Is there such a thing? Nobody knows for sure. In 1998, Scientific American ran a whole issue on oil. As I recall, one of the conclusions that they came to was that 50% of all the estimated oil in the world-not just the known reserves-would be used by the year 2000. They also said that the amount of oil being used every year was actually accelerating, and that when the oil so-called "ran out," people were saying, "We'll use natural gas."

"Necessity may be the mother of invention, but play is certainly the father."
Roger von Oech

The Russian scientist Dmitri Mendeleev, who developed the periodic table somewhere in the mid-1800s, was reported to have picked some oil up on his fingers and said, "Wow, this stuff is too valuable to burn." Well, we've been burning it ever since. Everybody may not know this, but no more than half of all the oil that's used every year is used for fuel. The other half roughly is used to make things: the pencils on your table, the paint on your walls, the clothes you wear, the laminated plastic in your kitchen, your cars, your fertilizers and pesticides, and a lot of your medicines. All these things are from petroleum. Not made from plastic, made from petroleum, from hydrocarbons. So things are a lot more serious than just running out of fuel. Hydrogen may not produce the same amount of power that oil produces, but it's still a very viable source of renewable energy. It's not going to make plastic, but plastic can be made by oils produced by plants like soybeans.

You might have to plant the entire United States with soybeans in order to get enough oil to continue going along the way we are. Let's just, for argument sake, assume that in fact oil is going to disappear. It may still be 10 years before rationing occurs in this country. It may be 40 years, but it won't be very long before the ocean of oil that we've been floating on, and depending upon, and have become completely dependent upon over the last 100 years, is going to be gone. So, what then shall we do? It's a very serious situation. Right now, something like $2.2 trillion a year in the United States is spent directly on the automobile, or indirectly through police, roads, cars, oil, gas, insurance, tires, and all this sort. This does not include accidents, and injuries, and death, and sickness from emphysema, from the fumes. It doesn't include any of those expenses. These numbers are just straightforward things that can be chalked up to the internal combustion engine in this country. Our military budget is way lower than that. Add up the amount of food that people eat in the United States, the military budget, all the food they spent, all the housing, and possibly the healthcare, and you still don't hit $2.2 trillion. It's an enormous amount of energy that's used in this country to keep this whole transportation system alive, and it's going to change radically, maybe not in my lifetime, but in the lifetime of any child born today.

So what is going to happen? This is a serious question that needs to be addressed. For years, I believed in polytechnics, which may have been an idea that came from Lewis Mumford. It is something we have used in building the biosphere and all of the other projects that I've worked on. Let's say you want to build a ship out of cement. You use polytechnics. You use the design of a Chinese junk, which may be 2000 years old design, and you might use aluminum masks and hemp sails. Or you can use something that just was invented yesterday. You don't need to feel guilty about using either one of them.

It's not a matter of going back-it's a matter of adjusting your life. It's what you do to be in a manner that can actually survive. Not just survive but have abundance within the context of however you're living. A lot of people think there are too many people in the world, about 7 billion people. I think that double that may be too many people. But if the allocation of resources was properly done, I don't think there are too many people in the world.

The Next Step:
From Biosphere 2 to Eco-Villages

Christopher Zelov: How long did it take for Biosphere2 to get off the ground?

Hawes: My recollection is that in about 1971, the man who is really responsible for the Biosphere 2 project, is John Allen. It was he who put a little thing up on the wall where he thought that if we did everything pretty correctly in terms of our ecological work, that within 14 years, we should be able to do a world-class ecological project. That was 1970. In 1984, the property was purchased to build the Biosphere 2 project.

Now, whether or not we did everything correctly in that area in 14 years, I can't say. At any rate, that always struck me as being very interesting that the Biosphere 2 project is not something that just some of us dreamed up, and you jumped into.

We didn't say "Hey, let's get a little gang of folks together and we're just gong to go build a biosphere." The people that built that had been working together, a large number of those people, the core group had been working together for 15 years. They weren't just suddenly deciding to do this project. You don't do major projects that way. It takes time. It takes time to be able to learn how to work together in a meaningful way. It takes a great deal of time and effort.

I think personally from where I am, that to go from the Biosphere 2 project into an ecologically sustainable village, is a completely logical step because the Biosphere 2 project talked about things like cycles, water cycles, sewage cycles, food cycles. How are you going to deal with a situation where you have water to think about? What do you do? How is your water going to be controlled? How do you deal with your wastewater, your sewage, and so forth? These are the lessons that I feel that I learned from the biosphere.

Also, about how unimportant it is for any one individual to be emphasized, how important it is for teamwork to be emphasized in major projects, and how the individual can float from one position to another, which I talked about a little bit earlier.

At Biosphere 2, we had people working on plumbing crews that were put on as leaders, crew leaders, who had never seen a pipe hardly, knew nothing about pipes, but were good crew leaders, and could learn. The most important thing was the desire to learn something, not what you'd already learned, and that you could learn to do what was of interest to you. If you're interested in it, you learn how to do it.

Zelov: How would you like your grandchildren to remember you?

Hawes: I think if my grandchildren remember me as that funny, crazy, old guy that was around and was a lot of fun and I liked being around him, that's how I want them to remember me. I'm not worried about being remembered as an architect or this or that actually.

Epilogue

We were talking about megalopolis, or what Patrick Geddes used to call conurbations, and where millions of millions of people come together, Cairo, Egypt, and Mexico City, and Los Angeles. You all know all those. The planners, city planners and architects, all went through planning graduate school and architecture school, and we think while we're in school that we're going to change things. Basically, I think, most people find out that when they get out of school and go to work, actually doing this sort of work, planning work, that the power structures of the community that is already setup usually controls where the sprawl goes. It's very, very difficult to work against that. It's very hard to swim up against that stream. That's why what I'm trying to do at any rate.

We want to have a fresh start from scratch on a new piece of property. This particular piece is a graded piece of property, which makes it even more interesting and more exciting. It's about 300 acres of our 630 is an old colici mine. It's been mine for I guess up to 60 or 70 years. We have the opportunity to do restoration ecology here. At the same time, we're covering up, building on something that is already degraded so we're not going out into the agriculture land and destroying that, but are able to work on property that needs to have human activity on it and human restoration work done.

At Biosphere 2 I remember we had people working on plumbing crews that were put on as leaders, crew leaders, who had never seen a pipe hardly, knew nothing about pipes, but were good crew leaders, and could learn. The most important thing was the desire to learn something, not what you'd already learned, and that you could learn to do what was of interest to you. If you're interested in it, you learn how to do it.

CHAPTER 3

The Creative Green City
The Lighthouse Project

Lori McElroy
SUST. Project Director

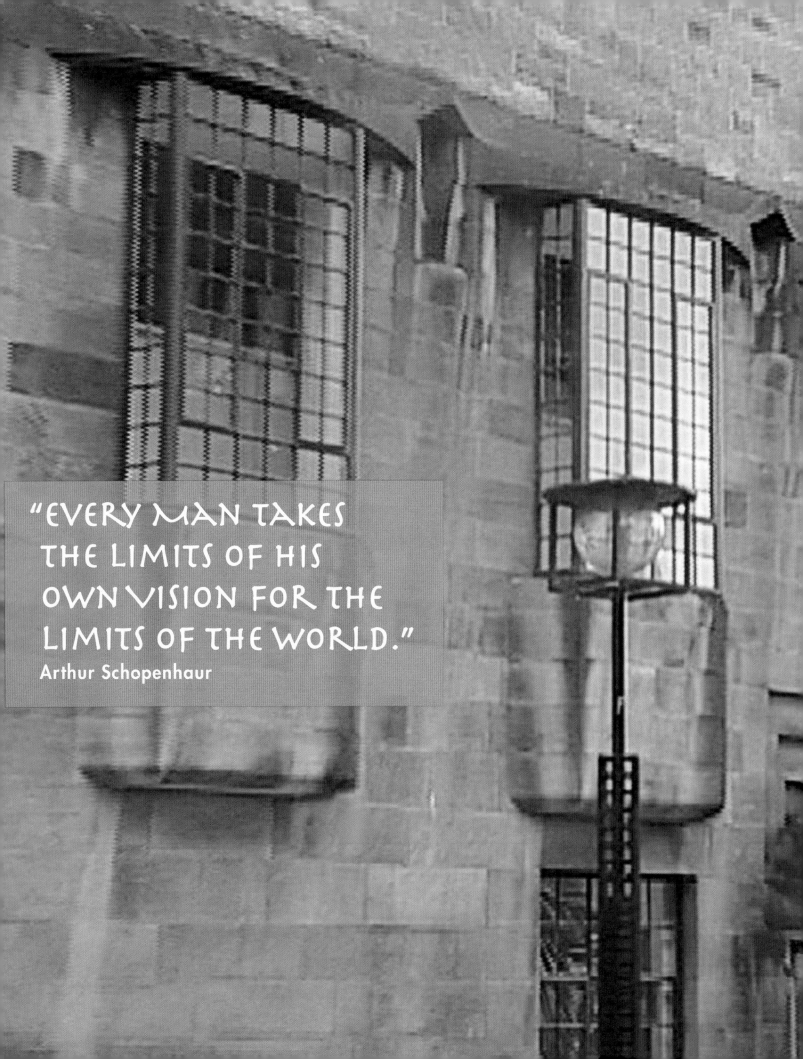

"EVERY MAN TAKES
THE LIMITS OF HIS
OWN VISION FOR THE
LIMITS OF THE WORLD."
Arthur Schopenhaur

As Sust Program Director Lori McElroy says: "we must learn to love the places we build in order for them to be taken care of through the generations."

Plato put it this way in 300BC, "Whatever a culture honors, it cultivates."

As their Mission Statement enunciates, the Lighthouse has an dynamic outreach mission. The Lighthouse Vision is: **"To be a leading body for the promotion of architecture, design and the creative industries, locally, nationally and internationally by engaging people of all ages through a creative exhibition, education and business programme."**

Indeed, bring heartthrob design to the people.

Make the rare ubiquitous.

Be a Lighthouse in the Sea of Time.

Exhibit the best design concepts from around the world.

Get people excited about excellence, if not virtuosity.

Build a community of design connoisseurs.

The headquarters of the Lighthouse, Glasgow, was designed by Charles Rennie Mackintosh, a leading light in the Art Nouveau period.

Why not now become a torchbearer in the age of green design?

In this interview, Lori further reveals some key aspects of this emerging Vision...

CZ

Chapter 3: Lori McElroy

Cousineau: Can you tell us about the beginning of your group, The Lighthouse?

Lori McElroy: The Lighthouse, I've only been here for about two years, but I was connected with the building a long before that. I can tell you about the history of the building. The building was the first publicly commissioned building for Charles Rennie Mackintosh when he was working with Honeyman, Keppie, architects in Glasgow. It was constructed in 1895 originally as the headquarters for The Glasgow Herald Newspaper. It remained in use as that until I think the late 1970s, early '80s, and when The Glasgow Herald moved out of here, and have since moved on again. This building was derelict I think from round about 1985. It was almost 100 years it was useful and then just short of 100 years, it fell into disuse and sat here for quite some time. The building's actually owned by Glasgow City Council. Glasgow was appointed as U.K. City of Architecture in 1999, and decided at that point to refurbish this building as a flagship project for the promotion of architecture and design in the city at that time.

Cousineau: Can you tell us about the significance of the name?

McElroy: The significance of the name for this building is connected with this tower in which I'm sitting at the moment. I think it was actually originally constructed as a water tower. There's, if you go up to the top of the tower, which is a journey you can make from the Mackintosh room, which is above us, and you can see all around Glasgow from that point. It originally housed a huge water tank and it is shaped like a lighthouse. It's like a beacon at the top of the building. A lot of others, this building was never really attributed to Charles Rennie Mackintosh, but in retrospect, looking at the decoration on the building, it would appear that the decoration suggests it is a very early example of his work. That's one of the key features.

Cousineau: Do you use it as a metaphor now for the work that you're doing in sustainable design?

McElroy: In a way, I would say yes, but not just related to the sustainability work that we do. The Lighthouse is here to promote architecture and design to the public, to a wide audience, to try to get the public to engage with

architecture and design. I think that you can't really disentangle that from sustainability because if people love the places in which they live, and like and appreciate the artifacts that they use, then they will begin to move and grow in terms of sustainability because we can become a less throw away and discarding type of society through this kind of appreciation. I suppose it's really based on the kind of Scandinavian model where everyone appreciates good design. The Lighthouse and the SUST program, which I operate, is actually a new addition to The Lighthouse. I think it should've been born out of bringing together all of the educational and exhibition, promotional and marketing activities that The Lighthouse has done over the last 10 years.

Cousineau: What's your working definition here of sustainable design?

McElroy: What's funny is it's a term, I know that if you use it in Scandinavia, they have great difficulty in understanding it because they tend to think of sustainability as being connected with more economic issues and they tend, for that reason, to use ecological design as opposed to sustainable design. For us, sustainable design, rather than using things that are fairly intangible like the Brundtland definition of sustainability, which relates to the state in which we find the planet and the way in which we should leave it. We tend to use sustainability within our day-to-day work as trying to bring together the three core elements of sustainability, in other words, the social elements with the environmental and the economic. This is one of the biggest problems, I think particularly for local authorities to try to bring all of these elements together when they're very much bound by the need for economic growth. That can't be done at the expense of the environment. They're good at picking up those two elements, but the impact of what they do, and from a social point of view in terms of creation of cohesive communities and lasting communities, I think is something which is maybe not always a pattern and which really should be brought out. I think another aspect of this, which I think is really important, is the fact that for me, sustainability, for a lot of people, sustainability is very much about a low-tech ecological approach. I think that we really have to also embrace the potential for new technologies because although they are really, really worried about climate change and global warming, if we very quickly back pedal and discard new technology such as renewable energy because we don't think they're efficient enough at this stage, or can send them to the back room because they're not ready yet. I think that we have been missing a lot of opportunities. I think that for the planet to survive, I know this sounds a bit emotional maybe, but for the planet to survive, I think it's very important for us to embrace hi-tech as well as low-tech solutions because I think that that's where the positive outcomes are going to come from.

Cousineau: Do you think that's what is possibly unique about The Lighthouse approach as opposed to the Scandinavian or the American approach? Is there a different attitude, a feeling tone towards the land here that might not be elsewhere?

McElroy: I think that in terms of, I think that we maybe sort of sit somewhere between the two because as far as the Scandinavian approach is concerned, they are very much connected with the land. They have not gone through the same kind of industrial revolution that we went through in the U.K. They didn't have the empire that we had and lost. They don't necessarily have the amount of baggage that we have. They make an approach people can tend to be quite critical of in this country in terms of lack of commitment to signing up to some of the global agreements. I think that there is also a growing swell in academic circles in the U.K. that say although there is clear evidence that the climate is changing, and that the planet is warming up, it isn't necessarily going to...I think that people in the U.K. tend to be, and particularly in Europe, tend to be slightly critical of the American approach, or in some cases, very critical because of the fact that they don't see America moving quickly enough to sign up to global climate change and environmental agreements. I think that there is growing recognition, particularly in academic circles in the U.K., that although the climate is changing, there is so much going on that we can't always guarantee that everything that we do is having as significant an impact as it might appear to be having. It might sound a wee bit cynical of me to say this, but there are a lot of people making a lot of money out of sustainability. There are a lot of people flying all over the world making money of sustainability, and probably causing more global harm than they would be causing if they were content to sit in their offices and video conference, but they like to go to the nice places to save the planet.
My reason for saying that is...

"DILETTANTE PERFUME BLENDERS, POKING INQUISITIVE FINGERS THROUGH THE GREAT LIBRARY OF INGREDIENTS AND SEEING WHICH COMBINATIONS MAKE SENSE FOR US--- GATHERING EXPERIENCE AND THE POSSIBILITY OF MAKING BETTER GUESSES, WITHOUT THE DEMANDS OF CERTAINTY."
Brian Eno

The key message from all of this I think is that the one thing that we all have to work with, whether we're changing the planet or not, and whether what we're doing is effecting the number of fish in the sea or spawning grounds, or whatever, is that we know that all of our resources are limited. At the end of the day, we only have one planet and so we have to make the most of the resources that we have. From an optimistic point of view, I'm actually quite confident that before we run out of oil, or coal, or gas, we will have alternatives, marketable alternatives in place. Although we are panicking about reliance, for example, on petroleum for car use, I think that the change is going to come quite rapidly because there's a lot of research work going on. I'm sure there are a lot of inventions out there, which companies are holding back on, and they're going to the marketplace when things get more even quite desperate. I think before then they'll start to filter in.

Cousineau: Could you list a few of the influences behind this kind of thinking?

McElroy: One of the key features of this building, of the refurbishment of this building, was to look at the opportunity for niche applications of renewable energy in the city. While we have a tower on this side of the building, which as I said already is sitting above us, which I shouldn't say in a film should I? The Lighthouse tower sits above us and gives a view of the city to the north. On the south side of the building, there is a new tower and a viewing platform, which is constructed entirely of glass, but which is self-sufficient in terms of energy, using roof-mounted ducted wind turbines, and floatable teak sales, and low technical solutions and high technical solutions in terms of the materials and the controls used, but all with a view to looking at the possibility from a city point of view of using renewable energy. One of the big criticisms of renewable energy is that you put wind farms in the countryside where people have plenty of energy and then transport that energy to the city. Whereas we have huge cityscapes with large roof scapes where we could be deploying all sorts of renewable energy that wouldn't even be seen by the public, and therefore could, from a planning point of view, easily be incorporated.

Cousineau: How about your outreach program? Do you have lectures going abroad? How do you reach out to children today, the up and coming generation?

McElroy: Our program, which is called SUST, just sust on sustainability, I don't know if you have the expression in America, but we have it. We run a program, which is aimed at getting sustainability to the public, to increase the demand for sustainability, and to assist with the mainstreaming of sustainability. For that, we draw on all the other programs within The Lighthouse. For example, we in The Lighthouse have the Scottish National Program for Architecture based here. We also have a very large education and exhibition program. We have a large conferencing team, who look after all of the facilities that we have here in terms of conferencing. We draw upon the resources of all of these in our program and try to feed sustainability into everything that we do. Some of the elements of our program in terms of outreach that might interest you are, for example, we have a children's game, which is called My SUST House, which is aimed at sort of age 9-14 children. It's just about to become part of the curriculum in Scotland. It is a game aimed at trying to not only raise awareness of sustainability because I think children get a lot of that kind of information at school, but they may not understand how to put it into practice. What we teach them about is a bit about the environment and the impact that we can have, the impact on where they live in terms of if they live in a rural community, the issues associated with transportation, going to visit their friends and those sorts of things, the alternative that they have opportunities to grow food and have renewable energy close by. We also look at the implications of suburban and urban living. They then go on to build sustainable house using everything from traditional materials like concrete to straw bales and tough roofs, but they have a budget. If they want to use sheep's wool insulation, they have to find a way of paying for it. They can blow the budget and that makes them think about what they do because if it we make, we can't make it too easy because kids are devious.

Cousineau: Do you know the American expression, "The tipping point," when enough people are thinking in a general direction then public sentiment suddenly changes?

McElroy: Yes.

Cousineau: Have you reach that in Scotland, where we've moved past the cynicism about sustainability and Eco-Design and the doomsday prophecies to a point where more people are now believing in the need for it?

McElroy: I don't think we've reach a tipping point, but I started in this area about 20 years ago. We were then trying to sell the idea of low energy design and energy conservation. At that time, people were skeptical about low energy design as they perhaps are now about sustainability. Over the last 20 years, we've seen a shift, not only in the general acceptance, and the breaking down of barriers, and moving toward a more sustainable and energy efficient design, but also an increase in demand to take things further. From sustainable, sort of from low energy design, we moved on to environmental issues, passive solar design, and renewable energy. Other issues like materials, particularly things like I mentioned, sheep's wool insulation, straw bale, these are actually becoming things which are not just one off demonstration projects are actually being used

in mainstream housing and social housing. There is a movement, but I don't think we've quite reached the tipping point yet. I think we've got a way to go.

Cousineau: We're all very interested in Ian McHarg. Are you familiar with his work?

McElroy: I'm not, no.

Cousineau: We were wondering if his influence has boomeranged back to Scotland?

McElroy: I don't know of him. It doesn't mean that, again I come originally from an energy background, so I think maybe the architects, those who came up through the architecture would might be more familiar with him than I am. Probably, if I mention this after this to them, they'll be quite disappointed that I didn't know.

Cousineau: Is there anything that you are incorporating from the ancient Celts, I don't know if you can go as far back as the Picts, or at least the old Scots, the way that people lived off the land for centuries to help with the turnaround today?

McElroy; Maybe not as far back as the Picts, but I think there's definitely a growing interest and a passion for looking at the use of local materials; maybe not going back to what we call the black house, which was built from stone and turf, and didn't have any windows, and had a hole in the roof for the heat from the fire to go through, but definitely the techniques of low housing in exposed climates, which pitch is which and more appropriate to the climate; those kinds of issues because we have tended to adopt a more universal, international style in the last 50 years or so. Other things that we're looking at from a more practical and up-to-date interpretation of all of that is to, particularly even with large scale commercial housing builders in Scotland, is to try to identify and work with local supply chain, not just local contractors who can provide materials, but actually the people who provide the materials for the materials, for example sheep's wool insulation. The bottom has dropped out of the (69:53) market in the south of Scotland. Yet there's no reason why we couldn't be using the sheep to produce wool, which is used for another purpose, in other words insulation. There are lots of opportunities like that. Even taking that much more up-to-date, you could envisage that although the bottom has fallen out of the electronics market to a certain extent, there's no reason why the same skills couldn't be used for manufacture of (70:20) and solar panels of other types. We have the skills. I think we just have to learn how to reinterpret and reuse them.

Cousineau: Can you describe a couple of minutes about something about the seminar you're going to in Finland?

McElroy: As part of our SUST initiative, we run a program called Sustainable Designs on You, which is a program, which is aimed at the social housing market, and particularly at housing associations. This year, we've decided to combine this, and maybe dangerously, with the large-scale housing developers in Scotland, commercial develops of housing because there is a move towards housing associations reducing in number, but taking on a larger remit. In order to deliver against that, they'll have to work more closely with housing developers. With this in mind, to make sure that it doesn't cause us to go backwards in terms of design, because our housing associations do tend to be fairly innovative in the way in which they design and deliver housing for the community. We're very, very community focused. In order to make sure that the alliance with the housing developers doesn't take us backwards, we're taking a group of housing association members, and developers, and architects, and planners to Finland to see the work that they're doing there, and also to an area just outside Copenhagen, and to Malmö in Sweden. What we're going to see there is how they've developed waterfront areas and some green space on brown field sites with housing development, which over there, maybe perhaps because land prices are much lower than they are in the U.K. because we have a fairly large population U.K.-wide for the area of land that we have. The contrast is that we have much higher land prices and we tend to pack as many houses into an area as possible. They value the importance of green space for recreational, but also for ecological purposes. We're going to look at how they deal with encouraging biodiversity, and also things like weed bed systems, and water based systems for dealing with gray water, and also waste water on site because this is a growing problem we have in the U.K. is that our drainage systems aren't able to take much more. We're just about up to capacity because the systems are getting quite old. We're going to look at those kinds of things. Also, and this is quite close to my heart because I come from one of the first new towns built in the U.K., and when these new towns were built, they were built as a kind of new model for living with not particularly high urban density, but a reasonable urban density, mixtuous in terms of people living and working in the same area, but also having plenty of green space for recreation and to make sure people could move safely between one area and another. One of the things that is happening now in the U.K. because of the pressure on land is that these green spaces are now being filled up with housing, and often housing which is not appropriate in terms of its relationship with the Elysian about. One of the key issues here, I think for local authorities, is that again,

> " THE ENVIRONMENT MEN CREATE THROUGH THEIR WANTS BECOMES A MIRROR THAT REFLECTS THEIR CIVILIZATION; MORE IMPORTANTLY IT ALSO CONSTITUTES A BOOK IN WHICH IS WRITTEN THE FORMULA OF LIFE THAT THEY COMMUNICATE TO OTHERS AND TRANSMIT TO SUCCEEDING GENERATIONS. "
> Rene Dubos

we tend to focus on economic progress and economic sustainability, but what they forget, I think, is that if you start to interfere with the social cohesion of an area by intensifying the number of people and depriving people of what was an amenity, even if it wasn't a very heavily used amenity, then you can create all sorts of social unrest. That from a sustainability point of view can lead to severe problems. That's why we're particularly interested in looking at what's happening in Finland. Another thing that I noticed when I was in Finland doing a kind of pre-trip visit, was the fact that because Finland is built on rock, or because Helsinki is built on rock, we were going and they tend to work with the land much more closely than we do. If, for example, a huge rock appears in your garden,

it becomes a feature. In Scotland, we would blast the rock and then sell it back through a DIY outlet for use in your garden. They tend to have a completely different approach to accepting that the land is the way the land is rather than trying to change it.

Cousineau: Would you say that something unique about The Lighthouse approach to sustainability is the social dimension?

McElroy: We use a term here, which I think we've adopted from the Netherlands, which is place making. I'm moving very much forward on a place making agenda. In Scotland in particular, it's become a kind of core element of sustainable communities. A key issue associated with that is that we are of the view, and of the growing view, and the academics are maybe of the view, but the public are of the growing view that you can create what might be called ecological or sustainable buildings, but if they're not beautiful buildings, and they're not located in beautiful places, then people won't love them. If people don't love them, then they won't succeed. From a social environmental point of view, you have to make sure you get that right. One of the key things that we're looking at now is improving the mix of people in our communities. One of the problems from a social point of view with what we call social housing or housing for rent, is the fact that they tend, people tend to live there until they can move onto something better.

What we want to do more of, and again, we feel that the Dutch and the Scandinavians are very good at this, is creating areas of mixed tenure, where people can live in a large house, which they've bought, live in a house, which they part on, or live in a rented house, which they either pay for themselves or is paid for by the state. If you create an area like that and you provide all of the other important amenities which are referred to, then you can

" DREAM THE IMPOSSIBLE DREAM, FIGHT THE UNBEATABLE FOE, STRIVE WITH YOUR LAST ONCE OF COURAGE, TO REACH THE UNREACHABLE STAR."
Cervantes/Don Quixote

encourage people, once they take a step up that ladder, whatever that ladder or how big that step might be, they can remain in the same community, but just move up a step and vacate that property for someone who needs to go onto that level. We're looking very, very closely at doing that sort of thing. Again, The Lighthouse's connection with the public, and this is one of the key features of The Lighthouse, there is a lot of architectural activity going on in Scotland. We have a body called Architecture and Design Scotland, who looks at the quality of design in architecture. We also have The Roland Corporation of Architects in Scotland, who is the body into which all of the architects subscribe, are members. The Lighthouse's uniqueness is this connection with the public and taking architecture and design to the people. Again, I think I mentioned earlier the fact that I think it's really, really important to take people along with you because if they appreciate good design, then they'll demand good design. Good design is sustainable. Not everything about good design is sustainable in terms of perhaps materials used, but if people love things that they have, then they'll keep them for longer. That's a step towards sustainability.

Cousineau: We've noticed that if you put up theoretical buildings that are ugly, the community begins to disintegrate. Is what you're describing part of that?

McElroy: I think very much so. I mean I know the old adage, a thing of beauty is a joy forever, is a bit of an overused expression, but I think it's coming back into fashion. There is another that we use here, which relates to this that is we're doing a study at the moment looking at a couple of particularly beautiful buildings, which I won't speak about just now. One of the things that we're looking at with them is what we call the forgiveness factor. If you give people ugly buildings that they don't love, then they reject them. If you give people beautiful buildings, even if there are things that are not quite right about them.

CHAPTER 4

Energy Independence
in
Iceland

Dr. Sigurgeirsson
Director, Forest Research

"WE ARE WITNESSES
THROUGH WHICH
THE UNIVERSE
BECOMES CONSCIOUS
OF ITS GLORY."
Alan Watts

Pertinent and cutting edge technology from the remote Island of Iceland?

The misnamed island, that should really have the moniker of Greenland.

Somewhat outlandish you might say.

Have you heard about the white gold of the north? Beyond the news of the recent financial meltdown, let's recall our real debt is to the Biosphere that sustains us, not the Banking system that contains us.

Tapping the renewable energy of nature serves the Long Now of a civilization that seeks a benign and enduring presence on Earth.

Indeed, the Viking spirit of independence from central authority resurfaces here in 21st Century Iceland. Despite the fact their ancestors may have disappeared into the mists of time and legend.

Their Gods may be unheralded. However, the modern day Icelanders are part of the emerging master narrative now shaping the World energy landscape.

As the Grateful Dead once sang: "You can't go back, you can't stand still, if thunder don't get you the lighting will." In the case of Iceland, both serve the co-creation of one of the key energies of the future: Geothermal.

Let's discover some glimpses into the unique dynamics of the Icelandic world with Adalstein Sigurgeirsson.

CZ

Chapter 4:
Dr. Adalsteinn Sigurgeirsson

Phil Cousineau: Can you begin by describing what the first settlers in the ninth century would have discovered here in Iceland? What did the island look like?

Dr. Adalsteinn Sigurgeirsson: All indications are that the island was forested for the most part in the lowlands, and that would mean that something between 30-40% of the total area of the country was covered with some kind of forest or woodland, the forest of just one species. There was just one species of birch that formed all the forests. These forests did not contain any grazing animals of any kind. There were no native mammals in the country at that time so these would have been very dense and very pristine in all manner of speaking. Pristine from the point of view that there were no humans, but there were hardly any animals either, apart from birds. What the settlers did when they came to this

country was what humans do in every society when forests are dominant on the land, they cleared for agriculture. They clear it to create pastures and grazing land, and in fact, most of the forests here wouldn't have been considered anything else than just an obstacle to settlement at that time. You find charcoal remains from that time throughout the country and all indications are that most of the forest was already destroyed during that first century of settlement. During the ninth century approximately, most of the forest was gone.

What the settlers also did was drive their grazing animals, their sheep and their cows, up to pastures in the highland meadows. What also appears to have happened in the first few centuries of settlement was erosion problems, land degradation problems in the highlands, which then continued toward the lowlands. By approximately the 15th, 16th century, during the start of the middle Ice Age, the land was already treeless for the most part, and was starting to erode, and the soils were starting to blow off. The soils were of volcanic origin and were very sensitive to any kind of opening of the land so they eroded quite easily.

After that, the population of the country dwindled. During the Middle Ages, Iceland suffered from various calamities, both disease as well as famine. The

> " MAN CANNOT DISCOVER NEW OCEANS UNLESS HE HAS THE COURAGE TO LOSE SIGHT OF THE SHORE."
> Andre Gide

famine was caused, to a large extent, by the fact that we had overstretched the carrying capacity of this country.

We had degraded the production capacity of this country and we were very sensitive to any fluctuations in our climate. During cool periods, during cool summers, they usually led to periods of starvation. If we had calamities like volcanic eruptions, which are quite frequent in this country, where ash covered large areas of the land and our grazing animals couldn't access grass for fodder, that also led to famine. During that period, Iceland's population continued to dwindle and this went on, this reduction in the Iceland population, until the beginning of the 19th century. What then happened was a series of more open contacts to the outside world, more trade, more fishing, and emigrations as well. What actually helped the Icelanders throughout that period was that they were very literate and they could easily adapt to new technology when it came up.

The destruction of the forest continued, however, into the beginning of the 20th century. By the early 20th century, we had less than 1% of the country covered with any scrub, birch scrub or wood. That is when the Danes came in. The Danes came in with almost, you might say, development aid to Iceland, to start some experiments with planting trees and planting forests. That took another 50 years, into the mid, you might say the mid-20th century, to convince Icelanders that trees could grow in Iceland. After you had managed to convince Icelanders that trees could grow, we also had to convince Icelanders that forests could grow. That only really occurred in the 1980s and '90s so we had actually a very short period of planting trees, of forestation in this country. Now it's well on the roll and we're planting more forests in this open, naked landscape than ever before.

Cousineau: Could you describe in a few sentences the Icelandic relationship to trees, does it stem from Celtic lore? Is there a mystical relationship with trees here?

Dr. Sigurgeirsson: We do have examples from earlier centuries of sacred groves and sacred trees in this country, very much related to both the Nordic, as well as the Celtic folklore, in that regard. I think that the human species itself has a very close relation to trees. Trees provide many benefits to humans, not only wood or timber or paper, but also shelter and bird life, and wildlife, and everything that we associate with being outdoors. Also, the tree is a symbol of a healthy environment. A healthy tree is a symbol of a healthy environment and that goes very much for Icelanders, just like any other people of the world, even despite the fact that we are in one of the most treeless countries of the world. The interest in planting trees is probably greater here than in most of the countries simply because of the lack of trees, lack of forests. We see this interest both in terms of participation in forestation in this country, where 20% of the population is active in supporting through opinion surveys, 93% of the population are positive towards seeing more trees in the Icelandic landscape, and 67% actually want much more forest and trees. There is a general positive attitude towards more trees, despite the fact that they were all raised and brought up in a very naked and earthen landscape.

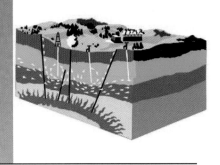

Cousineau: Can you describe the geothermal renaissance which occurred in the early 1900s?

Dr. Sigurgeirsson: We have always, of course, had geothermal energy and natural hot springs in this country, but these hot springs were not used apart from bathing in pools or washing pools. They found ways of actually using that hot water for heating houses in the late 1920s, here in Reykjavik. Reykjavik is located well in terms of hot water. There was hot water close to the town center. You could pipe it into the downtown center, but as Reykjavik grew, you had to go further away from town to find that hot water. There's ample hot water and geothermal energy in this part of the country, fortunately. That energy is used for heating almost all the households in the Reykjavik area. In fact, in 85% of households in the whole country, the geothermal energy is also producing electricity. The large proportion of electricity that's used in Reykjavik is actually from geothermal energy plants. The remaining electricity that's produced in Iceland is all from hydroelectric dams and hydroelectric plants.

Cousineau: Can you describe the renewable aspect of geothermal energy?

Dr. Sigurgeirsson: It's perfectly renewable in the sense that as long as we have volcanic activity in this country and we continue to have rain falling from the sky, we will continue to have hot water in the ground. It's not the case, as with fossil fuels, that you have to mine them and once the mind is finished, you've depleted the mine. It continues, the water continues to flow from the surface, deep into deep layers of the ground, heat up from the presence of lava, and then rise up to the surface, where it will be used. There is no reason to believe that even if we had a larger population and larger households in this country, we would run out of hot water or geothermal energy.

Cousineau: Can you talk to us about the character of Icelandic people?

Dr. Sigurgeirsson: Icelanders have been living in this country for 11 centuries, but we are very much still of a pioneer character. Our way of thinking is both from a point of view of a pioneer, but also from the point of view of a fisherman and a shepherd. We don't view things in a very long-term way, just as it goes from day to day. We've always had to live with uncertainties in this country and that's probably reflected on how we do things and view things. We're not a very good long-term planning society, at least not when you compare to our Scandinavian relatives to the East. We are more of a carefree people, which may reflect also our Celtic half, but we do tend to take things very differently from our Scandinavian relatives. We have a very closely-knit family society. We are very well aware about who are our relatives, what is the genealogy, and often discussion about matters tend more towards persons and people. Once you start talking about people, you start talking about who they are related to and so forth, rather than the issue actually at hand, go on to kind of a genealogical tangent in every discussion.

Cousineau: Does that also apply to how Icelanders feel they're connected to nature?

Dr. Sigurgeirsson: Yes. Our identity is very much tied to the land and the open sea. Fishing the ocean has always been a very dangerous struggle throughout history.

Cousineau: When you look around the world at the environmental catastrophes happening everywhere, do you see what you are doing here in Iceland as a model?

Dr. Sigurgeirsson: We are actually living in a country that you could certainly consider as much of an ecological catastrophe as the worse examples we have in our present world. Some Third World countries spring to mind, with their ecological problems of deforestation in Haiti, for example, or some sub-Saharan countries where forest and vegetation is lost both to man's overuse, overgrazing and then climate. We went to a very low stage in our history when almost all our forests were lost, almost half of our soils were lost, and almost all our terrestrial ecosystems were in very poor shape. Yet we found our way out of that to becoming one of the richer countries in the world as we are today. But we still haven't actually rehabilitated this country. We are finding methods and ways of doing that in a both ecologically and socially sustainable way. Many of the issues that we are facing in this rather rich country are the very same ecological issues that you're facing in the same, rather poor Third World countries in terms of land and environmental degradation from overuse, from agriculture. If you were to travel through Iceland and look at the country, it looks to be a natural, pristine, open landscape. No trees, no forest, no vegetation, you consider that just as part of nature. But the natural fact is that, this is an effect of humans. This is an anthropogenic effect like everywhere else.

Cousineau: We know Iceland is exporting its energy technology, in the old Viking spirit, by sending students, architects and foresters to other countries that are in trouble so that you can share the knowledge you have accumulated.

Dr. Sigurgeirsson: We are a very small society and therefore, to maintain a high level of education, we have for the last century, always had to send most of our students abroad, especially graduate studies at the university level. That helps us out also, our society, in that we are very open to outside influences from every part of the world. At the same time, as we maintain these contacts to the countries we go to study in, we also make ties with people from other countries. That is perhaps one reason why we are starting, increasingly, to export technology and know-how, such as technology for geothermal energy or for fisheries technology. On the forestry and land rehabilitation side, we certainly have potential, but there are very few of us in this country dealing with these colossal problems we already have. We would certainly like to see more ties abroad, as well in that field.

Cousineau: Jared Diamond in Collapse, describes himself at the end of the book as a cautious optimist. That's a fair statement for the state of the world today. Do you have some cautious optimism about the future, the future of this country, the future of the city, when you look at the patterns that are now in place?

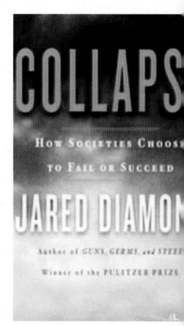

> "WE LIVE IN TWO WORLDS...
> THE WORLD INTO WHICH WE
> WERE BORN, AND THE OTHERWORLD
> THAT WAS BORN WITHIN US.
> BOTH MAY BE A BLESSING
> OR A CURSE. WE CHOOSE."
> Druid Homily

Dr. Sigurgeirsson: I would very much agree with Jared Diamond in considering myself a cautious optimist, but as I was saying earlier, Icelanders do not take a very long-term perspective. I have no grandiose hopes for my country for the future particularly. I'm fairly cautious, but optimistic. At the same time, consider this: just over 100 years ago, this was perhaps the poorest country in Europe. It was suffering from immense environmental degradation, immense emigration to, especially, North America. We had the greatest loss as a proportion of the total population, of any country in Europe, save for perhaps Ireland. Yet during one century, we bounced back into shape. I think that reflects a certain cautious optimism. For our country, which was facing such severe social and environmental kinds of problems only 100 years ago. This can be done, but perhaps the method is to maintain a certain social structure, high rate of literacy and outside contacts through other countries in the world.

Nigg

Balinto

Kilmuir

Firth

Cromarty

M

Balblair

George

eagle

ort

Nairn

Croy

Cawd

Kilravo

Building Eco-Villages

with the

Findhorn Foundation

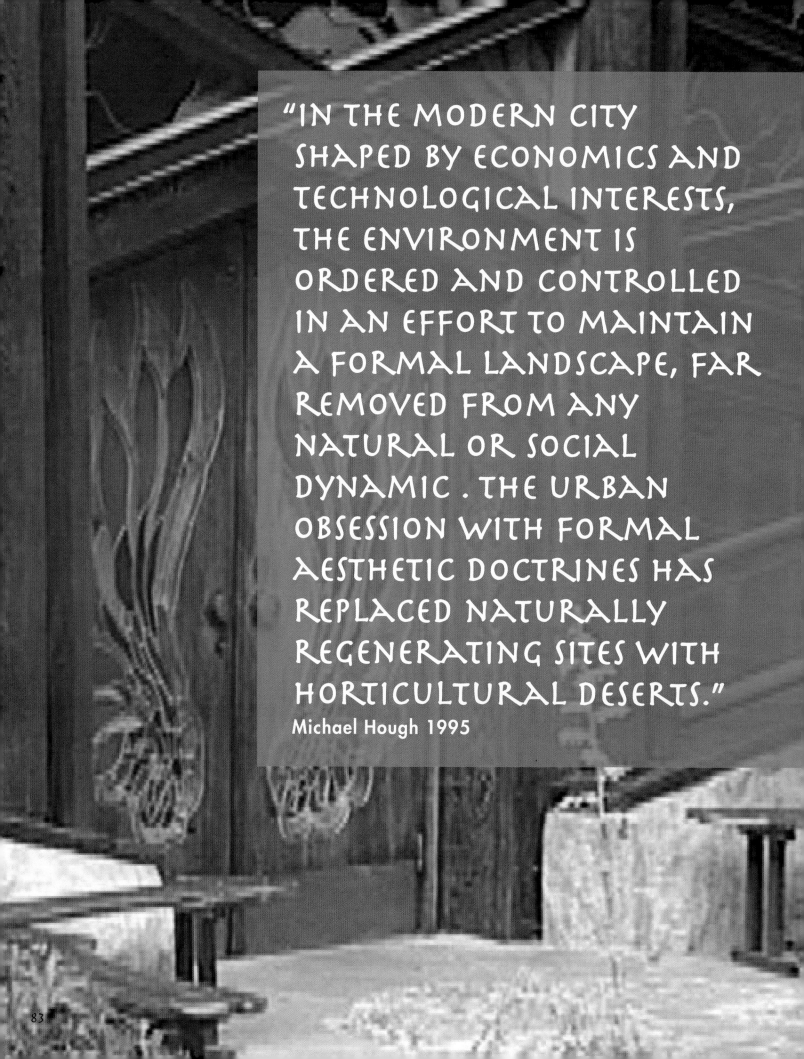

"IN THE MODERN CITY SHAPED BY ECONOMICS AND TECHNOLOGICAL INTERESTS, THE ENVIRONMENT IS ORDERED AND CONTROLLED IN AN EFFORT TO MAINTAIN A FORMAL LANDSCAPE, FAR REMOVED FROM ANY NATURAL OR SOCIAL DYNAMIC . THE URBAN OBSESSION WITH FORMAL AESTHETIC DOCTRINES HAS REPLACED NATURALLY REGENERATING SITES WITH HORTICULTURAL DESERTS."

Michael Hough 1995

Masdar City, Abu Dhabi

Findhorn is was founded in 1962, based on a particular Vision Quest, and then organically unfolding into an new ethos of settlement. Kick-started as a garden, it morphed into an intentional village for those seeking more out of life than provided in the confines of the industrial mindset.

Community member and writer Jonathan Dawson articulates: "making arts together is the glue that keeps the community going."

As Lao Tzu says in the Tao Te Ching:

"Love the whole world as if it was your Self, then you will truly take care for all things."

As we expand our definition of Self, we can participate with a new found energy in the co-creation of community.

Indeed, we learn from history, civiliztion arose because of the Agricultural revolution. Most communities were based on a profound connection to the land and were invented eons before the age of Petroleum. The Middle Age Village is a prime example of this model of human settlement (see Phil Hawes).

Amazingly, Findhorn is now a 25% net exporter of energy to the grid.

A living exemplar that shows it can be done.

When will other communities around the world find the social will to catch up?

The **Transition Town** and the **Net Zero** movement are part of the shifting consciousness in this direction. See the book by Rob Hopkins, and investigate Masdar City in Abu Dhabi.

Perhaps we must learn from Herbert Read when he reveals:

> *"The artist must penetrate to the source of the life force, the power house of all time and space, and only then will he have the energy and freedom to create with the proper technique a vital work of art."*

Above all, we need more artists mastering the realm of the Ecological Design, then perhaps we will find our way with requisite Elan Vital to a more bountiful future.

CZ

Chapter 5:
The Findhorn Phenomenon

A 4 Way Dialogue

Nature is ever at work building and pulling down, creating and destroying, keeping everything whirling and flowing, allowing no rest but in rhythmical motion, chasing everything in a endless song out of one beautiful form into another.
John Muir, Naturalist and explorer (1838-1914)

Tony Hodgson: The success of Findhorn has been widely recognized as one of the greatest modern successes in communal living. We're wondering how much it matters where we live, whether in a modern city, or in an experimental eco-village like Findhorn?

Yvonne Cuneo

Yvonne Cuneo: Yes, it matters whether people live here at Findhorn or in a city. By giving people in the major cities the chance to come and get in touch with what we're doing here, allows them to see how we're cooperating with nature. If they do surface, we can awaken something in each person who comes here, one by one. They're realizing that if we don't work and live in relationship with each other and with the earth, things are going to come to an end.

Jonathan Dawson

Jonathan Dawson: At Findhorn, the original idea was to train people to create eco-villages. The great majority of people who have come here have seen what's distinctive about an eco-village, and the way it all actually works.

Craig Gibsone

Craig Gibsone: I know the city can be a great place, and yet as I live here and I've seen so many modern cities turning pathological. Here at Findhorn we're having a coming together of the ecological and sustainability movement with a spiritual focus. So I question the viability of cities in the future. Of course, there are a few places around us here in the north of Scotland that are trying to work with small sustainable models, which may eventually fit into big cities.

I don't think the natural system can handle the demands of the megacities that will be coming in the future. Those huge populations will need deeper levels of sustainability embedded in them, instead of always just expecting the resources to come from wherever.

Cuneo: I came here for that deeper concept of community. I knew that what was lacking in my life was the nourishment of a community. I needed to belong to something intimate enough to feed my soul. Now, at Findhorn, we're questioning how big do we want to grow because we don't want to lose that original sense of intimacy. As for how cities can we create a sense of community I think it is by building a small amount of units within the city limits so people can feel known, can feel they belong, can feel an intimate relationship, and not feel lost in some concrete jungle.

Jonathan: Yes, I think that compact cities have every chance of being ecologically viable.

Creativitiy in the Community

" Given the trend of our age to eliminate the craftsman more and more, yet greater savings by means of industrialization can be foretold, though in our country they may for the time being still appear Utopian."
Walter Gropius, letter to the AEG company, 1910

Hodgson: Can we agree that another thing we're going to have to focus on in the future is the role of education in the community? We know that there is a wide range of projects going on here, such as the new arts center that's being planned. Isn't education a big part of what makes the community alive, expressive, even artistic?

Gibsone: For me, the interesting thing about creativity is that in our community is we have always attracted actors and painters and dancers and writers. In the early days we were always needed professional painters to paint houses - and we kept getting professional artists. There's a tremendous amount of desire within this community to create art, and I'd like to try and extend it because I'm a poet, I'm a painter, I'm all of those things. So I believe that art is a very powerful thing. We are all expressing ourselves here, which is probably the real glue of this community. If you look at it from the spiritual perspective, art is actually a dynamic, socially creative cohesion.

The Role of Beauty in the Community

"A work of beauty is a joy forever."
English proverb

Hodgson: What role does beauty play in designing your community, and its function in everyday life? Is it important or a luxury?

Christopher Raymont: I hope we are building a community where we're living together and allowing crafts to be a strong element in our life together. For me the beauty comes from our commitment to craft. When I look back over history it's clear that most people didn't have any choice about beauty and art when they lived in the city. Traditionally, people were probably surrounded by beautiful things they couldn't afford. But now that people can actually now afford a hand-made chair, it's in the mainstream, it's not just outsider people who are going for a very simple, a craft-based life. I feel it's an area where communities can provide answers because it's our function to offer enough people alternative set of values. Still, mainstream values are always coming in. That's a very strong feature of life here, so it's often hard to live that desire to have beautiful things.

"Nature is always mysterious and secret in her use of means; and art is always likest her when it is most inexplicable."
John Ruskin

The Influence of Oil

Hodgson: Now I'd like to offer you a kind of challenge: How can we afford the luxury of beauty and expensive designs when we're living in a world where oil [will soon be] priced at two hundred dollars a barrel?

Cuneo: To answer that, I'd like to offer the example of a hand crafted chair? Who can afford such a thing? Well, that issue comes up here. There is the man who makes a beautiful eco-kitchen for the new house of the man who, in turn, builds the foundations for him. Then there's the person who does beautiful stonework in return for another skill.

Dawson: We have a huge ensemble of talent here at Findhorn. When we offered training programs some years ago we wanted to include a performance artist and we followed all the good processes of applying for funds from the local council. In the middle of the training the local council voted for whether we'd get computer modules, Scottish harps, the theater. They voted marginally in favor, saying yes for all of the above. This is who we are and what makes community; this cooperation might be our most important technology.

Dawson: Many of the trainees who come to Findhorn expect the training to be predominately about windmills and other forms of hardware. Within a week or so, there's so much else going they get frustrated because there's too much holding hands and singing songs and not what they expected. But by the end of the month, pretty much everybody is in synch, which challenges most of their self-images.

Cuneo: The heart of what you said is that we need to have all our windmills united, our eco-technology in synch. But without the real heart in the community, the community is not going to work. That's where the sustainability is, in the heart. Without that we're just sort of dead shells.

"A hundred times I have thought, New York is a catastrophe, and fifty times: it is a beautiful catastrophe."
Le Corbusier, "New York: The Fairy Catastrophe"

Gibsone: If you look at the ways we create group synergy, you'll see that we work with conflict resolution and communication. If you come here without any skills, you'll actually walk out of the place knowing a whole series of exercises, dances and songs, which are actually deeply connected to your relationship with the planet and the sky. That is what people take away, even more so than with a memory of looking at our artistic sewage treatment plant, a living machine. It's actually the most beautiful place you could walk into. That's one way of re-consecrating our cities and communities- with places of beauty.

The Hidden Clues to Sustainability

"Building technology is a science, but the practice of it is an art."
A. Roderick Males

Hodgson: Could you pursue this a little bit deeper? Some of the more conventional work that I've been involved with includes thinking about people who've come to the unfortunate conclusion that we've already solved most of the problems of sustainability. But as you have been pointing out, we're not quite finished solving it. However, it occurs to me that this misunderstanding might be a kind of hidden clue to ways of enabling implementation.

Cuneo: We can all play lip service to the issue of sustainability. We can read books. We can talk. But until something shifts in people's attempt to fill their emptiness with buying things or filling their faces a sustainable world won't happen. Until people are living creatively, instead of living in fear, you won't be able to impose sustainable designs on them, saying, "Here are the technological answers-so now do it!"

Hodgson: Specifically, then, how do people move through your wider education process here? Do you have any feedback on what they undertake?

Dawson: If you want people to go out to sea, don't teach them to build boats. Rather, give them an endless longing for the openness of the sea. Have them build a shipbuilding factory. One of the reasons the ecological footprint isn't more impressive than it is, is that the people don't have a longing for a connection to the place where they live, a real love for the place.

Gibsone: One of the most interesting-and surprising-things about Findhorn is that we're not actually teaching technology to the trainees. We're always looking at their inner silence. I try to explain, "Let's forget the word meditation; let's forget the word spirituality." I say to them, "Let's just sit down and do a series of breathing exercises, just regulate our bodies a little bit, and see what we feel like at the end of the exercises." We have to do this because it's as if we just stopped trying to give the this generation the tools of how to cut a piece of wood, as well as the real tools of being comfortable within themselves.

Hodgson: What's the biggest challenge today with the relationship you have with the city?

Gibsone: I suppose my challenge with the city is that it keeps plotting to fool you back into the machine. My observation of all the students and guests who come here is that they're all slightly hardwired, plugged into a high frequency, a mode of constant moving. It's groovy and it's wonderful in some senses, but there's no space for silence where they coming from. Instead, there's a constant barrage of consumerism, telling them that they will be happy if they buy this, buy that. Whereas, at Findhorn, we're trying to actually tell people to just be happy with nothing. Maybe it's just about practicing silence.

Raymont: The combination of artistic eco-village and spiritual process is what makes Findhorn special, different than other communities.

Dawson: What we offer may actually be a subversive teaching, one that's a threat to this link in the Western mind between consumption and well-being. The great majority of people can never really impress anybody about their with own material wealth, and end up feeling that all they can see about life is that it is all about consumption.

Cuneo: The whole point is consciousness. That it's not actually what we do, but the consciousness with which we do it. That's what is going out into the world and it's creating your reality. Therefore, if you come from the email driven, frenetic pace of life, know that is pointless. Of course, we're not perfect here. We have problems here too and so it's always interesting to stand back and watch when our consciousness goes out the window. All the things that are related to eco-villages and sustainability and our relationship with nature will follow naturally from that. Each of us can only start with ourselves and help each other to do that. Of course, that's why Findhorn is an educational center too, because we want to try everything here ourselves. We want to help others find it too and so they go back out into the world and help inspire a global shift of consciousness.

New Pathways

"I honor beginnings, of all things I honor beginnings. I believe that what has always been, and what is has always been, and what will be has always been."
Louis Kahn

Hodgson: You've got an interesting design pathway here. You seem to be reconciling the eternal tension between individual freedom and community incorporation – in a dynamic way, considering how in the normal line thinking these are irreconcilable goals?

Cuneo: We're committed to serving the whole world with the understanding that sometimes we need to soothe ourselves in order to do that. Therein lies the dance; we are on the edge all the time. We do ask ourselves when is it self-indulgence and when is it actually serving ourselves in the healthiest way? When do I need to just step aside from that individual self (that's an illusion anyway) and move into doing what's needed for the whole community? When do we burn out? For me, this is actually the most fascinating aspect of life here.

Dawson: Besides trying to give people space to be silent we have sanctuaries all over the grounds, indoors and outdoors, so many you never know when you'll be coming across another sacred space. We have a great variety of choices. You can go around tasting things it's like a smorgasbord. Mostly, we have a meeting between the environmental and the spiritual. There is a very, very powerful energy of the soul here.

So much so you can say Findhorn is really about the transpersonal. When anybody is actually going into deeper inner space there is a spiritual emergence; something is arising, and we can use a series of tools to explain it and explore it.

Gibsone: There is always a collective will to try and hold on to your own ideas, and by the same format I'm totally relying on you to actually help create my community. So what is my responsibility to myself - and then to my wider collective? At Findhorn, there is an important element of what we call "the human scale." We think there is a deep desire in all humans to have an intimate relationship with maybe a hundred or two or three hundred people - that's about as much as you can manage.

Hodgson: It's amazing you can hold it all together.

Gibsone: People will want to be exploring that intimate relationship because the miracle is, how does everyone exist together here? We're a bunch of anarchists! We've all been on the streets and then we came here and we somehow agree to actually collaborate and try to live together.

Raymont: I still sometime wonder after coming back here if there is such a wild thing in terms of the social contract. The majority world perspective at this little bundle of industry and this appears to be the aberration. The more I think about it the more Schumacher was actually right. The scale must be small, small is beautiful, which is one of the reasons I'm here is at Findhorn, in Scotland. The heart of the success of our eco-energy experiment experience is that there are always some people giving to the community. Everybody can find a place of being tranquil and needed.

The Politics of Communal Life

"Critics are like eunuchs in a harem; they know how it's done,
they've seen it done every day; but they're unable to do it themselves."
Brendan Behan

Dawson: I'm compelled to go back to the subject of politics. My sense is that many people come here to get away from an urban lifestyle and they often stay for quite a long while. If there was a key thing I would love to see happen here it would be people taking responsibility or really having had lots of time for artistic work or spiritual work.

Raymont: At Findhorn, I've never worked harder in my life. But somehow I'm much more relaxed. I'm not going to pieces. The reason we all work so hard here is that we've come from a system that isn't working. So there's a greater balance now in the things that I do. If I'm in a real community I don't have to go back to a lonely flat and turn on the television and expect my batteries to be recharged.

The Findhorn Quality

Gibsone: The quality that I discovered in the Sixties is still here at Findhorn. While some of us may be stressed, we're actually creating an almost stress-free environment. Our participants and our guests and our patrons visit and often feel like they're walking into utopia. They tell us that they feel extremely nurtured. But I think we're actually not practicing our meditation enough. In the earlier days we did meditate a little bit more. Now, we've had a lot of anarchy about this. But I totally support practice; you practice when you can practice. For some, meditation might be mountain biking; for others it might be sitting in the sanctuary; for others it's cutting carrots.

Hodgson: How do you deal with the inevitable stress of living in a small community?

Gibsone: Of course, there is a certain stress that you get from living in a community where you know you're not totally isolated. There's a very good chance that when you are stressed that somebody will come to you and ask you how you're doing and whether you need anything. They'll ask, "How can I support you?" In the city, chances are you won't get that level of concern.

Raymont: The major challenge for everyone is how to create a stress free environment. Your internal stress and my internal stress will be there, but at the same time we've got this sense at Findhorn of being a kind of ambulance that takes care of people.

Skill Sets

"He builded better than he knew; The conscious stone to beauty grew."
Ralph Waldo Emerson

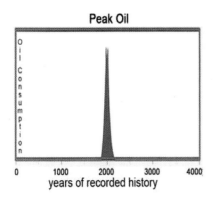

Peak Oil

Dawson: I have been watching the conversation, and there is this implication that normal society is over here and we're doing these funny things here. What I want to bring is that so called normal society is the product of this most abnormal blip in the availability of fossil fuels. How we live is much closer to, has much more in common with how we have lived long term as a species, than in the bubble. I like to think that what we're doing is keeping alive social skills, building skills, energy generating skills, learning skills. We're keeping alive the things that are really difficult to do in the bubble, so when the bubble pops, those survival skills will still be here. In terms of historical perspective, rather than saying, "Hey, what are you weird guys doing over here?" What we're actually doing is pretty close to using the skills that human beings have used for thousands of years, especially in terms of being self-sufficient.

25% Net Exporter of Electricity

Hodgson: Just how self-sufficient are you ?

Dawson: Early in 2006, we built three new wind turbines to add to the one that was here before. With these four now fully installed wind turbines we are now a net exporter of electricity. **We generate some twenty five percent more than electricity than we need.**

Raymont: I feel that we're trying to birth something new here, but not just here but throughout the global ecological movement. As Jonathan said, there needs to be a point where we don't have to manipulate and extract from my environment more than our necessary needs. Of course, you learn to say this from the point of view of the "three s's": soul, soil and society. You learn to show people that you can live more simply, and that you can definitely reduce your footprint or the amount of energy that you're consuming. This can happen in cities if we can restore the sense of the village inside in them. But it seems like cities have swallowed us like giant amoebas. They're just growing and growing and covering over all these once lovely little villages that had the butcher, the baker, the candlestick maker. I have a feeling that part at some point that small-scale life will return in Schumacher's sense because that is what actually feeds the heart and the soul, at least as much as my MTV.

"The city should be an organization of love…
The best economy in cities is the care and culture of men."
Lewis Mumford

Is it Real or is it Matrix?

Gibsone: It is challenging to imagine myself in a twenty year old body where the amount of energetic information that is been binding me the whole time until I'm a robot and don't see the world around me anymore and seeing only this virtual reality. To jump back to a so-called simple lifestyle, where all that is not taking place is hard. Hopefully, Findhorn-style eco-villages and spiritual centers can be places where people can step outside of or unplug from the so-called real world and enter into this, which is really the real world. At Findhorn, they can unplug from the hardwired world and take their shoes off and climb a tree or light a fire and come back to their cellular memory or their biological soul. Until we balance our cellular world with our immense intellect we'll continue to destroy the habitat that actually we're dependent upon.

"The town is new every day."
Estonian proverb

The Soul of the Place

Gibsone: When I was in a Tibetan monastery I was introduced to the possibility that humanity has become the soul of the planet. Now we talk about the souls of cities and this or that community. Eco-villages are tiny experiments where that soul becomes slightly recognizable. Cities are the big challenge. In New York-wow- there's such a powerful soul in that city. There's a chance that within that soul people will come to see the city as more of a living being that it has to be healthy to really thrive. The city has to have actually more space, more flower gardens and edible vegetable gardens. If we don't touch the earth, the soul of the world will continue to be out of bounds.

The Living Machine Greenhouse is a really beautiful place. But what are we co-creating with there? It's not just the pipes and plumbing. There's a whole history of evolution in there. One of the journey's I like to take, is to go into the greenhouse, and as you step across the threshold, you are stepping across the first wave of extinction. From the anaerobic to the aerobic. I am part of that memory now. There is something that trying to happen where humanity is sensing that it is part of the biological chain of existence. From an eastern perspective, they'll talk about reincarnation, from a Western perspective I would talk about cellular memory. My cellular memory jumps my ancestors and it jumps wide across the spectrum. Then you're all of a sudden into a realm, which is akin to primordial thought, perhaps shamanic. It seems at this point, we have forgotten that we have access to the intelligence of GAIA. In some sense GAIA is speaking through us.

I like Bucky Fuller's reference to the planet as "Spaceship Earth." But we have to learn to fly it or fly within it. The message would be for us to see that we are suspended in space and we should feel more a part of it. The ecological sort of devastation that we're creating [could] reawaken that sort of biological soul within us as we see further and further destruction. When things change the cities will find it harder and harder to have the necessary energy that they need to exist at their level.

The New Planning

Hodgson: We'd be interested in hearing is your views on whether the eco movement, which is clearly gathering some energy, will ever connect in any significant way with the mainstream? Will it ever influence the traditional way of planning and managing our communities?

Dawson: It's clear that the core impulse of the village movement is its utopian aims. The eco-village movement is looking at the mainstream and saying that that society is so badly

off track and moving so much in the opposite direction in terms of how, for example, it's educating children or treating the natural world, that we will need to choose consciously to step outside the system and model something completely different. The core impulse at Findhorn is strongly utopian and consciously alternative, with very few connections to mainstream society.

Now, it seems to me, the most important trend we're seeing at the moment is that it's changing and changing fast. There are a growing number of connections between eco-villages and more mainstream institutions. There are two main reasons for this. The biggest one is that mainstream society is recognizing that the communities movement are pioneers who called it right. Local Government authorities are being given Agenda 21 targets to meet and they're going, "yikes, we don't know how to do this." They're looking at eco-villages and seeing that actually eco-villages have pioneered techniques for reducing food miles, for managing wastes sustainably, for creating community currencies, and producing renewable energy.

Over the last fifteen years, it's become progressively more difficult to create communities. This has to do with legal fee's, rapid increase in land prices, tightening planning regulations, ever-greater individualization of society, which makes it diffulcult for people to commit to community.

I think simultaneously communities are looking at local authorities and saying we need help. We need help in terms of you integrating us into your planning initiatives. For example, here in Scotland we have petitioned the Scottish Executive to include a planning catagory for eco-villages within the legislation. The petition so far has been sympathetically received.

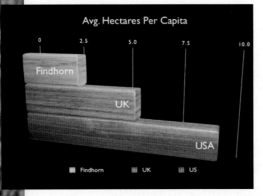

Instead of seeing Findhorn as a weird bunches of strange people, the government is now looking at serious experiments in living much more lightly on the Earth. Here at Findhorn, our recent ecological footprint results have shown that our footprint is half of the national average. This is a substantial result and its drawn attention.

The metaphor I like to use is that eco-villages are like yogurt cultures. There is a dense composition of a very live virus. The task we are recoginizing is that we need to infect the surrounding area with the virus of sustainabilty.

Here at Findhorn, we get almost 4000 guests a year coming through our training programs. That's a combination of spirituality, arts, crafts, ecology, and sometimes a fertile mix of all three. We punch way above our weight in terms of impact. If you took an aerial photograph of the North of Scotland, you don't even see us. However, in terms of developing a model and then using education as a means of communicating this, it's proven to be very succeesful indeed.

Un Initiative

Hogdson: What's the significance of this new connection emerging with the United Nations?

Dawson: A step in the way was the development of a program in the USA called Living Roots. Which is a program that provides students at American Universities with the opportunity to study at eco-villages for credit. We're one of seven eco-villages around the world. I teach a course in applied sustainability.

Then Findhorn won a UN Habitat award in 1998 for best practices. Since 1999, our eco-village training has been formally accredited by the United Nations Institute of Training and Research (UNITAR). The exciting development over the last two years is that educators from eco-villages from around the world have been meeting around the theme of GAIA education. This is an attempt to distill eco-village experience into one common curriculum dealing with among other subjects, ecology, arts and crafts, spirituality, and world views. It's also been adapted by UNESCO as part of the UN decade of education for sustainability. The future direction will be to explore with Universities to see if there is a demand for us to develop a degree program.

CHAPTER 6

Magical Architecture with the Damanhur Community

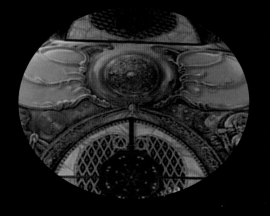

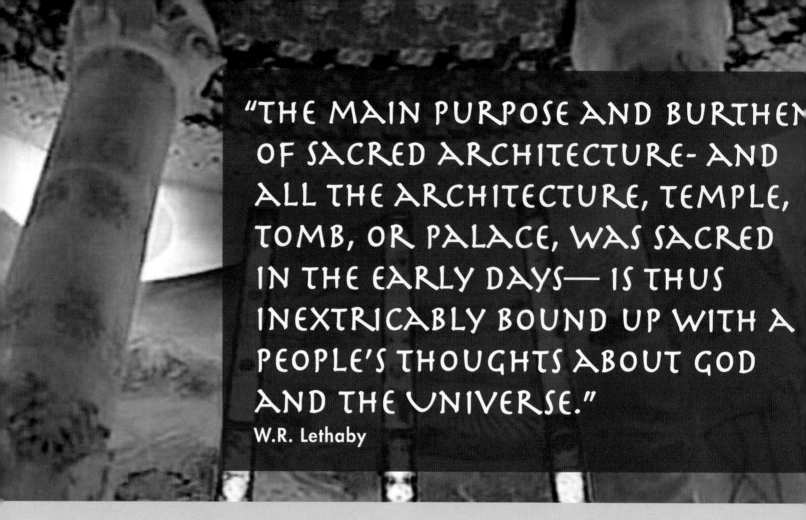

"THE MAIN PURPOSE AND BURTHEN OF SACRED ARCHITECTURE- AND ALL THE ARCHITECTURE, TEMPLE, TOMB, OR PALACE, WAS SACRED IN THE EARLY DAYS— IS THUS INEXTRICABLY BOUND UP WITH A PEOPLE'S THOUGHTS ABOUT GOD AND THE UNIVERSE."

W.R. Lethaby

The federation of Damanhur is an intentional community situated in the ancient Piedmont landscape, just outside of Turino, Italy. A captivating place where bringing forth an Allegorical Architecture is a part of the living fabric. Allegorical Architecture, or the Architecture of Parable, is part of a long didactic tradition.

Journeying back to the cryptic Luxor Temple in Egypt. Around to Delphi in classical Greece. Up to Rosslyn Chapel in Scotland. Across to the Antonio Gaudi designed Park Guell in Barcelona.

These are stunning exemplar's where ancient wisdom is subtley encoded within the site plan. Indeed, one has to learn see with a decoding lens, in order to glean the knowledge.

The underlying intent of Allegorical Architecture is to reveal a way of relating key elements, forming corresponding structures that transmit knowledge. In such (magical) constructions, there are elements that are purposely introduced to confuse the observer, while others are positioned at pre-arranged points to serve in the delicate transmission of knowledge.

When and if the Architectural program goes beyond merely programmatic demands, then the composition may open the door to the more elegant and lofty features of human existence. For instance: Art, Philosophy, Science, contact with the divine, interaction with other planes of reality, can all be fused within the scope of the symbolic stage set.

We live in a pluralistic Universe, as Renaissance philosopher Giordano Bruno articulated:

"There are infinite number of Universes, each possessing a similar world with some slight differences-a hand raised in one, lowered in another-so that the perception of motion is an

act of the mind swiftly choosing a course among an infinite number of these 'freeze frames' and thereby animating them."

Indeed, Damanhur is a avant-garde interpretation of what a City of the future may become. A place where the divine light within is cultivated and sought. Where the art of building is practiced with spiritual intent. Not dissimilar to the Masonic concept of the the inner and the outer tower. In line with the Gospel of Thomas, but not the Gospel of John.

As Theodore Rosak wrote in his classic book:

Person/Planet, after our democratic rights, we also need the right to Personhood. A self-discovery and inner liberation ethos, and the right for all the institutions of society to support the exploration.

There is a Greek concept called "synoikismos" —it has something to do with the spark of City-Making. The echo of which has reverberated through the corridors of time. Perhaps Damanhur is a "synoikismos" that can light some new time travel corridors leading to a more fulfilling City World.

Let us recall, the landscape of urban America was gridded before it was fully explored.

The gridded City can be deconstructed and re-weaved in blue/green terms. Indeed, the future inner/outer form of urban existence is an open space for re-invention. I see places like Damanhur as incubators, and beacons for an expanded cultural Ethos that can take us to next stage of human evolution..

CZ

*Sacred Architecture reflects a Cosmology:

- The World Fabric

- The Microcosmos

- Four Square

- At the Center of the Earth

- The Jewel Bearing Tree

- The Planetary Spheres

- The Labyrinth

- The Golden Gate of the Sun

- Pavements like the Sea

- Ceilings like the Sky

- The Symbol of Creation

* From: W.R.Lethaby: Architecture, Mysticism, +Myth ©1891

Chapter 6: Magical Architecture with the Damanhur Community

Cousineau: What makes Damanhur project unique?

Falco
Founder of Damanhur

Falco: First of all, for the American public, what has to be imagined is that this is a new frontier. Today, Europe is a new frontier. That which is happening to a beautiful place way back in the conquest of the lands is happening now in the opposite direction here in Europe. More than a conquest of land is a spiritual reclaiming of the inner territory. Since the '70s, this was a very fluid land to welcome changes. The lack of the government's ability to embrace change gave us the opportunity to bring the ancient back to the new.

DAMANHUR
The Subterranean
Temples of Humankind

Cousineau: What I see here is a convergence of history, and the future, and a convergence of art, spirituality and architecture. What is the importance of having such a variety of perspectives?

Falco: We have to start from the very basic point that difference is wealth, while uniformity impoverishes, and diminishes wealth. It's like an ecologic system where there are a variety of species, the planet is healthy. When species diminish, then the planet becomes sick. This happens also to the human species. As we are losing animals and plants species, so we are losing languages, we are losing cultures, we are losing people. An experience like this one tends to demonstrate that people not only disappear, but they also tend to form themselves again. At Damanhur, we have formed a spiritual people.

" POETRY IS THE KEY TO THE HIEROGLYPHICS OF NATURE."
David Hare

Not a biological people, but a spiritual people. To increase the wealth of the planet, to increase the complexity, we have to increase the differences and value the differences right now, at the very moment when so many people and the species are disappearing.

Cousineau: In Jeff Merrifield book about Damanhur you are quoted as saying that people can "retrace the pathways back to the divine."

Falco: To us, the divine is inside each person. To us, the divine is not more present in one person, than in another person. The only difference in people is that some people will

actually seek this wealth of the divine inside, while others don't. Instead, they seek out pleasure through things, and not wealth through the spiritual arena.

Cousineau: How do you move from inspiration to actually building? You seem to be able to trigger in other people something that encourages them to act, to take risks, to use their imaginations freely.

Falco: This thing has to be faced accordingly, especially by looking at the languages. For example, in business, in the productive activities, the language is motivational. For a businessperson to have his company work, he has to motivate and he has to have his people believe the direction that he is going in. That's one language. The thing is that they are no dependents here. I always say Damanhur is a community of individualists. The highest wealth is when people can attach their own personal dream to a train of dreams. When there is a push and the train is moving, each dream pushes the other dreams. I started the locomotive going, but without the passengers, it would not have gone anywhere. It's a dream that has to be nourished by facts because dreams for us are real when they can become something. They are not real when they stop at walls of reality. To us, to do is the spiritual thing. For us, if it was a religion, we could say that prayer and doing was the same thing. This is the mechanics.

Cousineau: What models from your reading of history did you have in mind when you began planning this community? Do you envision being a model now for others in the future?

Falco: I didn't want to follow models. I just wanted Damanhur to be an original experience. It is sufficiently so, not completely, but sufficiently so. The direction is there. We have tried, we have dreamt together. Now, we have goals that we are going to try to reach that are even larger than the ones in the past. Let's imagine Damanhur is a machine. We have spent a lot of time building this machine and to learn how to drive it. Now, the machine is made, the pilots are there and we can start moving quickly. For us, the future dreams are quite evident. They are part of a dream that is now becoming real through built things. We have started to prepare that which will be the new temple. It will have a dome of 5500 square meters. It's not just to build another temple. It's to show how something abandoned like an old quarry can become something else, in this case a temple. It's one of the main goals that we are going towards, and there are many others. In a very little while, we are counting on having a completely self-sufficient energetic power, as well as self-sufficiency with food.

Cousineau: It is interesting how the history of the construction of Damanhur is displayed here. On one wall are photographs of the exterior of Damanhur, illustrating the solar energy systems in place here. On the other wall are photographs of the actual digging into the earth to create the underground temples. Exterior on one wall, interior on the other. It is reminiscent of the German Romantic poet Novalis who said, "The soul is there where the inner and the outer world meet." Together, there is a vision of true sustainable architecture.

Falco: There cannot be a differentiating.

Cousineau: Is this a useful metaphor, to think of the temples here at Damanhur as a way to sustain the soul as well as the community?

Falco: Do we then need a place to care for the soul and the mind? I'm reminded of the words engraved into the entranceway of the original Alexandria Library in Egypt: "The Place for the Cure of the Soul."

The idea of the book, the idea of the written word is the transcript of life.

Cousineau: There is a tremendous spiritual hunger for these kinds of words, languages, communities all over the world. Do you have advice for people who are looking for a different way to live?

" IN SERVING EACH OTHER
WE BECOME FREE."
King Arthur

Falco: If I can give advice, I would say, do not consider spirituality just commerce, a trade. Do not consider the spiritual search something that you take, and then put away and then pick up, and put away again. If we think of the spiritual research as a commercial enterprise, we will never be able to then find the real thing. I also advise people to avoid the easy self-absolutions. It's not enough that people decide once a year to send good thoughts for the peace in the world, for example. It's important that our spiritual pursuits become a form of art: the spirituality of doing and creating. That's my advice.

Cousineau: For the past few years we have been interviewing designers, architects, futurists, teachers, artists and asking them what they recommend for a better future. If you, Falco, can imagine a better New York, Sao Paolo, Rome— what would it be ? Would you bring more Art, make it easier to fashion beauty. Damanhur is so spectacularly beautiful, we're wondering if beauty itself is part of your vision?

Falco: I see the cities with much less surface, being more underground. All of the surface that is being used for homes, etc., it makes you lose things instead of gaining. Services on the surface and to live in beautiful, very appropriate types of environments underground, so that there are gardens on the roof. Rooftop gardens become more and more ubiquitous.

Cousineau: How did ancient Damanhur, in Egypt, inspire your vision here in Italy?

Falco: The ancient city isn't existing anymore. Right now, is just a gritty industrial city. In ancient times, it was a city that was preparing the magicians of the future.

It had an underground part, both the geographic aspect and the spiritual aspect. Our inspiration came from there.

Cousineau: One of the powerful symbols from the ancient world is the Holy Grail. In the original telling of the story, it is only the knight with the pure heart who is allowed to actually see the Grail Castle. Were you thinking of the Arthurian Legends when you were constructing your underground Grail Castle, so to speak?

Falco: I believe the Grail is more than a myth. The difference between myth and reality is that myth remains just an event, while reality produces real things, facts. Whatever myth that is at the origin of history, origin of culture, if nourished, becomes a reality. This means that in Damanhur, we have the Grail.

Cousineau: Another way of talking about it, is that Myth isn't true or false, it's either dead or alive. Do you feel what you have created here at Damanhur is a kind of living mythology for those who live here, a sacred story to be part of?

Falco: Damanhur is a living story because it has a thirty year history. It's a point of inspiration for those people that come here. That's its job. There are many roads that can be walked. We began with just a small number of people, and with very little economic means; but we were able to create a beautiful underground temple. Others can do the same. Damanhur's job is to show pathways, and to show people that they can do more than what they think they can do.

Cousineau: What is the role of initiation here? Does it help people to think of themselves as an initiate in a mythic story?

Falco: It's the only way to really be there. Being an initiate means that the person is able to connect the physical part with the spiritual part. It's the whole person that you should seek. There is not only one truth, obviously. There are interpretations of the concept of truth. At Damanhur, we have only one dogma, one point that is still, unmoving, and cannot be changed. It says that everything can change, which is the opposite of dogma.

Cousineau: Anthropologists describe how the initiate moves from one level of consciousness to another, higher level. That may be one way to think of the temples of Damanhur. Initiation isn't a flat, one dimensional journey; it's a three-dimensional journey, which is different than a steady progression.

Falco: There are the levels, they aren't all the same. People aren't by nature the same. They can excel in some fields and be defective in others. In a balanced society, there rests the chance for people to excel in whatever they can excel in regards to others, compared to others. It's part of the spiritual place to have a point of self-realization from each person. The balance is done through all those things.

Cousineau: When you were constructing the Temples over that period of 20 years, were you mindful about the association with the Paleolithic caves, of France and Spain? Some scholars believe they were not only galleries of beautiful art, but caves of initiation?

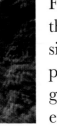

Falco: Yes. All that our ancestors did was well motivated. It's obvious that there are parts of those galleries that are like the sanctum sanctorum, similar to the central part of the Egyptian temple. One must navigate a path; it's a goal that, little by little, one is pressed to reach. It's part of the game of initiation to be able to journey through the caves, to get to the end. In our case, instead of finding caves, we are creating them.

Cousineau: That is a playful way to regard the caves and temples. Recent research tells us that people learn more when there is a sense of play.

Falco: If education is fun, they learn. If it's not, they unlearn.

Cousineau: Could you speak briefly about the role of play at Damanhur?

Falco: For us, play is fundamental. It's what allows us to experiment with new things and ideas, for example, if someone has an idea of living in a different way in a place. People go and try it out. If they have fun, if it works, they continue. If not, they change.

Cousineau: Is there anything that has surprised you about this 30-year experiment that you did not expect?

Falco: Every day, there is something that surprises me. Otherwise, I would be bored to death.

Interview with: Esperide Ananas

Cousineau: Why is it important at this stage in the history of Damanhur to let the world know what's happening?

Esperide Ananas: If you allow me, I'd like to reverse the question and ask why it's important for the world now to know about Damanhur. I think that it is because we can provide an experimental model to find new ways of living together as a community, of spirituality applied in everyday life. Indeed, in a ways that has been tested now for thirty years. I think we can be a good model for other people that want to try and create something new. We believe that it is not necessary to always follow in the footsteps of others, but it is possible to be creative, not only creative in the performing arts, painting and poetry, but in being creative first of all with our life.

Cousineau: Can you extrapolate on that? Why does this combination of art, spirituality, and architecture, work so well?

Esperide: I have a background in politics, and for several years I was the assistant to the vice president of the European parliament. Then I moved to New York and earned my master's degree at NYU. While in New York, I had the chance to consult for the United Nations on issues that had to do with development. Then I came here to Damanhur. I can say now that in my experience, this is the most advanced experiment with new social, economic, and artistic ways of living.

Why is this working? I think one of the reasons why Damanhur is working is because Damanhur is always changing. We constantly change. We know that when we have a model that's working very well, that's the time to change it. You can only improve, you can only evolve, if you're able to bring change forth at the level of maximum momentum. If you wait for things to get static and decay, then it gets very difficult to change them and improve them. Change is normally thought of in society as a way to fix things. We think that change is the way that life is. Change is life itself. You change things when they're flowing, when they're going well, so that you can reach new levels of awareness. When this movement is collective, what you can obtain is an imaginable force.

Cousineau: If it is so effective and natural to change, why is it so difficult?

Esperide: I find living at Damanhur very satisfying and I know that everybody who is here feels the same. It is also a big challenge for us, because in the West, we've been brought up thinking that in order to affirm ourselves, we always have to do it at the disadvantage of others. Even if this is not said openly, this is really the atmosphere that we breathe. So competition is always pushed to the limit. That makes it very difficult for people to understand that competition is only a good thing when it's done for the good of everybody. I think this is a difficult thing, for many people feel that in order to be themselves they have to forget others. At Damanhur, we believe that in order to be fully ourselves, we can only do it if we are in a group because then your uniqueness can stand out. How can you know that you're unique, if you're alone?

Cousineau: Still it can't be easy for people to live together. As you told us before, it's easy to romanticize life at Dahmanhur. What are the challenges that people face who live here?

Esperide: In the outside word, it is normal to get used to things, to develop a habitual way of living. At Damanhur, there are constant reminders and constant stimulations not to get mired into habits. Constantly choosing things, you can develop a habit, but then there comes a time in which, if you really want to be aware of your life, you've got to choose it again. You may see that your life works, or you may see that you want to change it. This is what makes it a challenge, because it is not the normal way of things to be constantly changing and reinventing oneself.

Cousineau: It must also be a challenge to emphasize the beauty of living in the moment, while at the same time holding an ambitious vision for the future. How do you balance those two viewpoints?

Esperide: Generally, we believe that in order to achieve great things, you've got to have impossible objectives. If you are only satisfied with what is possible, then you only achieve average results. If you really have a vision which seems impossible, then you can reach results that will surprise you. The temple here at Damanhur is a good example of this. We built it like this and it happened because nobody told us that it was impossible. Now we have people all the time coming to Damanhur all the time and asking us, "How did you do this? This is impossible." Well, thank you for not telling us before. We didn't know we couldn't do it and we did it! I think this is a combination of holding a great vision and living the moment. You have a dream that's so impossible that keeps driving you more and more, and then you take little steps and you're very aware of your little steps. For instance, in Damanhur, each one of us keeps a diary so that we can constantly see where we are in relation to our dreams. We have a great vision for the future, but also a constant foot in reality.

Cousineau: Henry Moore, the sculptor, said the same thing. He was asked about the secret of art and he said, "You have to have an impossible task in front of you and do it even though you know you can't possibly accomplish it. Then you do it anyway." To think like an artist may be a way to appreciate the dream that's come true here at Dahmanhur. Can you help us understand the spirit of collaboration here?

Esperide: This aspect of the arts is very important for us. Again, I have to speak of the temple which is really a collective work of art. The temple would not be possible if that were the result of just one person's inspiration. It's impossible. We believe that the gift of each one of our artists can be enhanced by the fact that they're working together. It's like the sum of their uniqueness. In the temple, in the hall of the earth, the ceiling took 15 months of nonstop work, 24 hours a day on the scaffolds that were 8 meters high. Everybody who lived at Damanhur those years participated. For us, that's really the symbol of what you can achieve when everybody puts their energy, imagination and will power into the things that they do.

Cousineau: When I was in the temple I sensed a kind of architecture of the soul.

Esperide: Actually, at Damanhur, we have a very architectural idea of the soul. We believe that we have a divine spark, and around it, a series of personalities. The new person, which is me, which is you, living your life now, is the new experience, but to help us, we also have other people. Really, each one of us is a group, and this is one of the

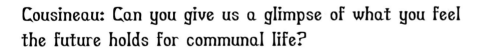

reasons why it's so important at Damanhur to reflect yourself in a group: mirror yourself in a group. Because the people outside of you are actually reflecting the people that are already inside of you. When you learn to live in harmony with those living around you, you also learn to live in harmony with the ones inside of you.

Cousineau: Can you give us a glimpse of what you feel the future holds for communal life?

Esperide: One thing that I think would be very valuable for the world to learn is that you can really let go of fear. When you live together like this in such closeness, with impossible goals ahead of you, you really see that everybody is just like you. Everybody has got their joys, their strong points, their limitations. If we're all the same, there's no reason to be afraid of each other, there's only reason to help each other grow.

Cousineau: When you explore the Temple there seems to be profound correspondences with the body.

Esperide: Yes, there is a correspondence with each room in the Temple with an organ or a part of our body; and of course, it also represents the human soul. Again, because it is dedicated to humanity, and right now, we are in this world of forms, we believe that we are the bridge between the material and the spiritual plane. The temple reminds us of this. We have a part that is linked to the physical manifestation, which is the manifestation of the forms of the divinity that we are, and then of course, many, many layers of metaphors until we reach the highest metaphor of humanity as a divinity, manifested fully.

Cousineau: Since living in Damanhur have you become more optimistic about the future?

Esperide: By nature, I am an optimist. I always choose to think that there are solutions, possibilities and new ways to explore. Yes, living here has helped me, because I've seen how much I have changed, how much I have become more aware, happier, and I would say with more energy and love for life. I think that if it worked with me, it can work for anybody.

Interview with: Gorilla

Cousineau: Can you tell us how the ecovillage fits into the Damanhurian philosophy?

Gorilla: An eco-village means to live in symphony with nature. An eco-village fits into our philosophy, because it is about living in harmony with each other that reflects the symmetry of the natural world around us.

Cousineau: Do you feel like what you are accomplishing here, what you are living here, is a possible model for the future of the world? Is it possible for other people around the world to live like this?

Gorilla: I think this philosophy of life, which is not anymore only a dream, but it is really a concrete part of life. The way we are living here could become a model for communities around the world.

Cousineau: What is the connection in the group that keeps you living on the land with such equanimity?

Gorilla: The spiritual part and the details of daily life are fundamental. Spirituality is the glue of life here; it makes your life more dense and that means that you can arrive at really higher, superior levels of life. We are living in this beautiful place for about 20 years. When we arrived here in this place, things were really different than they are today. This was an area which was completely abandoned by human beings. There was no road, no water, no electricity, only a few houses. In those years, we did a lot to make this a beautiful place to live. We tried to have contact and harmony with nature, and we tried to use the resources of the nature. We have a little aqueduct, which feeds water to all the houses in the area. The wood that we find around here helps us to heat the houses all year long. Thanks to the solar equipment we are using also the power of the sun to produce warm water and electricity. We are demonstrating that it is possible to live together and to have communial aims. To share all this, to arrive at these aims together, gives you a real inner spiritual growth. We hope that this point of our dream can be a stimulus to other people that are looking for a type of life like this.

Cousineau: Do you believe you have found the difference between searching for paradise and creating paradise?

Gorilla: To create paradise is for sure a very interesting point, because to understand that paradise is something that you can create is a thought that takes you close to the divine. I hope and wish that every human being on this planet is able to create his own paradise.

City 21 – Interview with Possum

Cousineau: What is it like to be an artist at Damanhur? What is the role of the artist here?

Possum: I think the role of art in Damanhur is as an instrument to bring out our inner divinity. We use art as one of the forms, one of the instruments that we use together to make this big alchemical popular operation, spiritual operation, and is one of my best personally. Personal, spiritual and mystically, art is surely part of my humanity. Art is spiritual action, an inner action to give significance to things. For us, giving significance to things, giving meaning to things, is a divine expression, which all human beings can do.

Cousineau: Still, there are communities all over the world involved with spiritual, political, or social isues. What makes Damanhur different? Possum: I think because art is that specific ingredient to help make a spiritual people, even magical, as when you make apple pie and need apples. You could not make a spiritual people without art. That's why we make art all together. Everyone contributes their skills to the creation, thus forming of a big collective prayer; that makes the end result endowed with much more power.

CHAPTER 7

The Utopian Imagination with the Open City Group

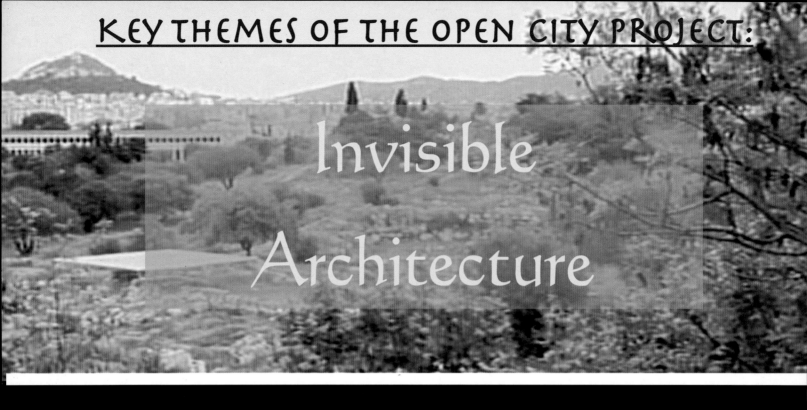

Invisible

Architecture

Volver

A No Saber

Poetry &

Architecture

Utopian Imagination

America as a Gift

The Interior Sea

> "A POEM IS A PHOSPHORESCENT INSTANT ILLUMINATING TIME."
>
> Laurence Ferlinghetti

Open City is one of the most unique avant-garde architectural projects underway on the planet.

Avant-Garde in the sense of pushing the edges of what architecture is, and how it is brought forth in the world. Penetrating the veil that encrusts the rather encoded and tradition bound design process. Apropos of that recognition, we learn from English writer Ruth Eaton* that there are at least two historical approaches to Ideal City design:

1. Platonic—
   Pre-existing form, or ideal form.
Describes what is seen not only by the physical, but by the mental eye. It designates a general or Ideal Form, an absolute pattern, the eternally existing and purely intelligible essence of the sensible things in the ordinary world we inhabit, while the latter derive their existence from these archetypical ideas and are but imperfect copies of them. In other words, Universals, not particulars.

2. End of the 16th Century onward—
   a more relativistic conception.
Any product of mental apprehension or activity, existing in the mind as an object of knowledge and thought. Open to all, a somewhat democracy of Ideas. Indeed, an elite profession of City Planning would arise in the 20th Century, and shape many of our cities.

*Eaton, Ruth, Ideal Cities, Thames & Hudson, 2001

For a myriad of reasons, what post 16th Century planning turns into is the formulation of urban space that is determined by an imported formal program and the classical principles of grid, axis, plaza, court, periphery, linear movement, object in field.

The Open City Group has introduced a *think different* approach to this age old modus operandi.

More akin with German composer Friedrich Schiller, when he states:

> *"Art is the free play of the spirit bringing into being what could not be have been predicted in advance."*

This is an Utopian project, as co-founder Juan Purcell articulates, they strive **"to invent a way of building what they want, when they want."**

Deploying Poetry to conjure form, they seek to unhinge the dominance of geometric metaphors on the nature of Architecture thought that becomes shape and substance.

To further quote:

> *The poet was an alchemist who employed the imagination to transform reality both mentally and physically; who embraced the mystery and adventure of creative activity as reality was opened up to different reading, a different understanding, a different reality ignited by the unifying body of poetic language.*

This kind of perspective was further elaborated by the Italian playwright Luigi Pirendello, whose work investigates the subtle ways fiction and fact blend to produce a continuum of verisimilitude.

A witches brew of truth and illusion. For example you say? The formulation of a World System. The imperiums of Christianity, Capitalism, Islam, and Nationalism, for instance.

The Open City approach is about a reawakening of the creative urge to find freedom in building a world based on our deepest desires. New vistas and plateaus are being revealed in the poetic mind endlessly. These poetic acts of imagination can bring forth unparalleled worlds. Tune in and learn to re-tweak your environment with the Open City philosophical framework.

CZ

Chapter 7:
The Open City Group

Phil Cousineau: We discovered you the hard way, in a book, The Road That is Not a Road, that we found in a bookstore in San Francisco. Now that we're here it seems like your "Open City" is a kind of City that is not a City, a Utopia that is not a Utopia. Everything here seems counterpoised to something else. How is your idea of utopia different than the other utopias in history?

David Jolly: Our way of utopia is formulated by the poet, Godofredo Iommi, as an espejismo, "a comparison with reflection." Iommi called it the vision you have in the desert, something you may see that it is not there, but it is somewhere else. What Iommi says is that it is a reality that is thinner; it has one dimension less than other utopias. At Ritoque, that "dimensionlessness" in our architecture means that we know what we've built is not going to last. We build things here not even thinking that they are going to last for a long time.

Juan Purcell: We just were in Bolivia discussing this idea of utopia. The principle thing is that the word utopia means "no place," which is something that cannot exist. But we insist that utopia can exist. That is the main problem in understanding us. The proof lies in what we have actually done here. That is, we think Ritoque is a kind of utopia because we are actually building the ideal. That's the only way that the utopia can exist. It's not only something you imagine. You can also build what you can imagine. We are proof that utopia can exist. This is the espejismo, the theoretical background of the fact.

Cousineau: Your form of utopia seems to be located in the present moment, the intensity of the poetic act; it's as if you're saying that utopia can only be built if we meet the ideal conditions, or if we are the ideal.

Jolly: Of course, yes. Utopia is always present, always possible, when you are aware of your origins. So you have responsibility to honor your origins. For instance, the way we live in the Open City is marked by hospitality. The poet Iommi says the way we are going to live here is with hospitality towards others who visit and between ourselves. You must practice it every day. The difficulty with utopia is that it is usually formulated for other people. To finish with this espejismo, this utopia at Ritoque was not formulated or imagined or designed to be done by someone else-this utopia was designed in order to be done by us.

"The gift must keep moving."
Lewis Hyde

Cousineau: In the West, land is often considered little more than a commodity. But the view of the Open City is far different. Is it influenced by the way you look at the land itself, as land as a gift?

Jolly: Yes, because an American point of view is that America is a gift. That's our real origin story. We don't have a formulated myth in America, as Europe has the myth of Europa, the way of Europe. What we have here on this land on the edge of the ocean is a gift, because this was not a discovered continent, but one that appeared in the middle of the long route to India. That's our sign, the gift. Iommi also looked at the oddity. At the Open City, we believe you must always be looking at the oddity, the unusual, the exception. That's what keeps you going in the proper direction.

Cousineau: The psychologist Carl Jung said whenever you're in crisis as an individual or a culture, you should go back to the beginning because that's where the energy is that you need to keep going forward into the future.

" NATURE IS A PETRIFIED MAGIC CITY."
Novalis

Purcell: Yes, because the beginning is what you cannot change. You may change everything else, but not the origin.

Cousineau: Is this what is meant at Ritoque as "buildings as inhabited poetry ... the dream of Ritoque's world renowned school of architecture."

Jolly: Yes, we are all involved with poetic architecture-what we received as a heritage from the French poetic spirit of Baudelaire, Rimbaud, Breton, the Surrealists, Whitman, we all studied at one time.

Cousineau: Now you choose other Poets. The French Surrealists for example?

Purcell: All this started from the meetings of an Architect and Poet in the 1950's . They began to talk to each other, and other artists, and they formed a group. They started to talk about the present, the new world. Every one of them remounted their own heritage. We also received the heritage of Alberto Cruz and Godfredo Iommi founded in the origins of our culture, Greece, Italy, France, and all this confirmed in them our own

heritage. So we didn't elect the Poets; the Poets chose the Poets.

Cousineau: How do you struggle with the tension between the people wanting to build something that will last, and your concept here of dealing with the ephemeral?

Purcell: There are two kinds of cities: the old European cities, that last a long time, Rome for example; then there are the Aztec cities that lasted only one generation. So every generation had their own cities. It's another point of view. America says something different than Europe about that special theme.

Jolly: It's also a poetic point of view. The poetic Vision of Amereida is not trying to change everyone's life; we want to change our life. If you want to change eveyone's life you must deal with power, if you want to change your own life, it's an artistic possibility, you can do it. We may live in an ephemeral building, but we don't pretend everyone does it. It is just an artistic possibility.

Cousineau: Do you see the role of Architects changing as we move to the future?

Purcell: I think Architects are just slaves to the Poet. They must listen to the Poet and do what they can do.

Cousineau: When you describe trying to be sure that you're helping students to see in the right direction, it is very interesting to us as foreigners to see the metaphor is to turn back to the sea instead of to face the continent. Can you help us to understand the idea of turning back towards the continent of America?

Purcell: Because we think we live in the borders of two seas, the Pacific and what we call the Interior Sea. That's the center of America, which is the most unknown part of America. The unknown. It is the future in a certain way, that's why we always live in the borders looking to the Pacific and we travel to the interior, to the interior sea.

Jolly: There is also another dimension to Architecture. Normal Architecture these days is very much standing on use, not standing on the vacuum to be reality. So when we founded the Open City, we wanted to develop some spaces to live that were not founded on the use, just standing in front of the original landscape, making the work of Architecture reborn from this interior. That's why when you visit the Open City, you can see the original landscape.

Cousineau: Can you help us understand the power of the image of the Southern Cross and why it is important in your mythology?

Purcell: The Southern Cross, in the first place, makes us look to the sky, that's a very important thing. The Southern Cross became a sign in the sky and also an orientation, the same as the North Pole star. That's our orientation, the Southern Cross.

Jolly: Also in the poem in which we are founded, Amerieda says something about the Southern Cross, because in the Southern Hemisphere and in America nothing can be directly transported. We were discovered by Europeans, and nothing is exactly transported from Europe to South America. The sense of the orientation is different, the Sun here comes through the North and in Europe through the South. Also, the stars in the heavens, we don't have in the Southern Hemisphere a Polar star, but we have what Magelan noted was this Cross. It's far from the Pole, it's a reference and it moves through the night. The poem refers to the Southern Cross as a sign of our possible point of view.

Cousineau: Speaking of the poem "Amereida" can you tell us the role that it plays in the Open City, especially how it is possible that the "word" can build the world?

Purcell: That's not a very new thing, because all America was built around the word of the Kings of Spain and England. Now, we think that there is another America that can be built through the work of poetry, the poetic word, thats another word play, that comes after the word of the Kings.

Time and the Art of Architecture

"It's packed with magic."
Open City student

Cousineau: Great ideas take time, they're beyond time. The ideas at Ritoque seem to be architecture's equivalent of the "slow food" movement. So is it more difficult for you to teach these ideas as the world keeps moving faster and people become more impatient? Is it harder to reach students with these "slow ideas" like poetry and time?

Purcell: I think every time, every era, has its difficulties. I don't think we have a very special difficulty now. There are always difficulties with this kind of teaching, and thinking, and living, and building, especially with a project like an "Open City." There are always difficulties, because the world doesn't go in the same way from generation to generation-it goes in another way. So you're always going against the stream or the current.

Cousineau: But the one thing that doesn't change is the beginning.

Purcell: No, the beginning doesn't change. Some people look and hear the beginnings, and other ones don't look at it and they forget it. We think that they get lost.

Cousineau: It sounds like you're trying to shape destiny itself.

Purcell: Yes, of course. Destiny is the principle thing that you can complete in your lifetime. You can accomplish your destiny. That's the main focus of every man, every city, every continent, every race, every culture, every everything. To accomplish your destiny!

Cousineau: Does a city or a community have a destiny as well?

Purcell: Yes. The city is the total destiny of all the people who live in the city.

Cousineau: You cite Alberto Cruz, in *The Road that is Not a Road*, that the destiny of the Open City is the destiny of Valparaiso.

Jolly: Valparaiso is being lost, because it is going up into the hills and losing its connection to the sea.

Purcell: Yes, that's a different interpretation.

Jolly: That special mantra is about the city of Valparaiso as a city standing on the coast in order to have the port, the relationship to the the sea. Urbanistically, though, the city has lost the relation with the real shoreline, because the city built the railway, and now uses the harbor as a place for stocking containers. Metaphysically, the city has lost its form because the airport is related to the sea; and no one can reach the sea now, because it's all used by something that could be somewhere else: the airport.

Valparaiso has two options to grow. One option is to climb the hills. The other option is going around the valley, which is an easier way of growing. Valparaiso opted for growing along the valley beside the river that goes to the inside of the region. We are proposing the other option so that Valparaiso continues its growth up into the hills until it reaches the summit. We are proposing a housing project up there for about 100,000 people.

Politics

Christopher Zelov: Are you able to engage the politicians in this?

Purcell: The university can study different projects and can propose ideas; that's its job. The ministries must do their thing. What we can do is to think about the destiny of Valparaiso, and propose the best plans. Every year, we work with a new group of students to offer new plans. Right now, we are proposing a plan along a very special avenue of Valparaiso that's called Avenida Brasil. But we're always proposing something to a city.

Zelov: Throughout history, the city center has been considered its very heart and soul. But how does Valparaiso maintain its center as it keeps growing up, up and away?

Jolly: The center is always changing. There's no one center now. There are many centers in every city of the world. You can't identify a center with a plaza now or a square. That's the old city plan.

Purcell: Yes, the new city center of Valparaiso is not the plaza anymore. Now it's the seashore. We have some special streets that go from the plaza to a station in some cases.

Designing the Conversation

Zelov: How is the communication between Valparaiso and the Cuidad Ábierta? Has a design conversation developed?

Purcell: Many of our students work in the city and then go forward with what we are thinking when they become architects of the local government. There are so many things that our school has thought in different times, have in a certain way have been built in a certain way, not exact replicate something embryonic, since it can start things.

Cousineau: I wonder if it's possible to have a common horizon between Open City and Valparaiso?

Purcell: The Open City is a part of Valparaiso. We don't think we are something apart. I live here in the Open City and I go to work to Valparaiso twice a day. I go back and forth so the city is today with the speed of, how you say, the mechanic speeds is a bigger concept. It's a lot bigger. It's not just the local downtown where it was founded as a city. Nowadays, it's much bigger. We are a part of Valparaiso. The Open City is the place where Valparaiso thinks about the way America could be built.

Destiny or Destination

Jolly: Of course, we belong to Valparaiso. That's a fact. We have a special destiny with Valparaiso, and we must try to ensure that this vision of the destiny of Valparaiso can be transmitted to the people who are in charge of building the city. That's our aim. We think every city belongs to a continent, and in a certain way, all cities are related to each other. They are not isolated, every city in the continent. It's not a question of building here and this is a kind of fortress alone, just standing there. No. They form a big drama, or a network, with all the cities. We are thinking for all of them. It's a common destiny of America, especially Latin America.

The Agora

Cousineau: I've always been impressed by the central importance of the agora in ancient Athens. Can you help us understand the process that takes place at your agora, half a world away from Greece?

Purcell: Of course, we took the name agora from the Greeks. We did not invent it. But it was the most appropriate name for what we wanted to do. Agora is what we named the place where we hold our reunions or meetings.

Jolly: When the Open City was founded, the first construction that was done here were the agoras. The founders built two or three agoras because the poet Iommi said that the city started with the agora, which is the place where we rule ourselves. No, we didn't start with houses, but with this public place, the agora.

Purcell: Yes, because the way we rule ourselves is by consentimiento, with consent. That is to say we don't vote. We all agree.

Jolly: Yes. Someone proposes a new building, for instance, and if one of us doesn't want it, we cannot do it. It's difficult.

Purcell: That's why we talk so much.

Jolly: Yes. That's the way we rule ourselves-everybody must agree. Otherwise, we don't do it.

Purcell: That's why we talk. We must talk very much. We must not just change what we want to do, but adjust what we want to do so that everybody agrees with the proposal. That takes a very long

"THE GROSS HEATHENISM OF CIVILIZATION HAS GENERALLY DESTROYED NATURE, AND POETRY, AND ALL THAT IS SPIRITUAL."
John Muir

time.

Jolly: It takes time. In a way, you must reveal what you really want to do because when

123

someone doesn't agree, it's usually because there is something that is not clear.

Purcell: Everything is related to origins. It is not so difficult. For instance, if we want to create a new piece of artwork, a new place for the theatre, we "do an agora" if we want

to to build it. If we are going to change something, we "do an agora." We have no police. If we agree to do [build something] and someone doesn't do what we want, we may tell them there is something wrong, but we don't have a repressive way.

Cousineau: Do you ever feel vulnerable to the outside world?

Purcell: That's it. The Open City has no defenses. We are very vulnerable in the inside; we are very vulnerable on the outside. Of course, if someone comes in and steals something, you may call the police. But there is no poetic police here.

Zelov: There's no censorship?

Jolly: We don't live with that.

Zelov: Frank Lloyd Wright would be very happy with you, one of his dreams was every man become his own cop.

Challenges

Zelov: What is the biggest challenge for you?

Jolly: What you hear sounds nice, and sounds very beautiful, but it is really hard to maintain, and manage. It's very, very difficult.

Zelov: What is the hardest struggle in moving the dream forward?

Purcell: I don't think we have big challenges. Our dream is that every day we can do what we want to do. The difficult thing is to notice the plentitude we have in the present. That's difficult.

"THE POETRY OF THE EARTH IS NEVER DEAD."
John Keats

Zelov: One of our honorary mentors for this project about the future of the city has been Buckminster Fuller. He spoke forcefully about the choice we have in thinking in terms of abundance or in terms of scarcity. Do you think we actually have a choice anymore?

Purcell: No, we have no choice. We must do what we can do with what we have. We

cannot choose to make a building with expensive or difficult to find materials; we use what we have, some wood here, some sand there, and stones everywhere. We do with the money we can collect between us. There's no yes/no choice there. It's not a materialistic choice; it's a philosophical choice. You see the plentitude of what you've got - or you don't see it. The plentitude doesn't depend on that one facet.

Zelov: Is solar energy a discourse that you're involved with?

Jolly: We have a philosophy that anything we want to do can be built with any material that we already have. We must invent how to do what we want with what we have. That means low technology, or very unsophisticated materials. That's the main thing. The important thing is that we can manage to do what we want in the moment we want. That's amazing.

Zelov: Do those resources come from a common pool?

Purcell: Yes. They come from where we can manage, from different resources and very different ways. The object is what we want to do, not the way we do it.

Zelov: Less is more.

Jolly: Yes. Exactly, that's very nicely put. Less is more, yes.

Zelov: You do have the sun.

Jolly: Yes, in the future, we must elaborate the energy of the sun.

Zelov: If the gringos from the North said, "We'd like to give you solar energy."

Jolly: We'd be very happy.

Zelov: About this choice of materials, that changed throughout the years? How did that happen?

Purcell: We started first with wood, because the cheapest material is pine. It grows very fast in Chile. It's a cheap material. Also, because when you are thinking from this poetic fundamental, something you aren't working with it's blueprints you say? We started building something; we didn't know how it was going to end. It was the combination of those two dimensions, cheap and also building it board by board.

Cousineau: It sounds like Robinson Crusoe.

Zelov: What about vernacular architecture?

Purcell: With most buildings, the architect draws the plans. Meanwhile, the building is a matter of the engineers and the contractors, but not of the architects. It is not inhabited. What we try to do in the Open City while we are building the building, is something you may inhabit. Building with wood is a good thing because it allows us to correct the form as we build it. So it's a living process.

Twenty years later, wood has proved not to be as good as other materials, because you must dispend lots of work in maintaining it. Also, it carries the risk of fire, and it does not have good insulation. We are always testing what materials would be the best for this work. We don't have an ideology of materials, so we must do everything with this. We build buildings one by one. It's an equation, a very complex equation, a problem to be solved as we go along.

The Metaphor of the Dunes

Cousineau: Can you talk about the sand dunes as a literal and as a metaphor?

Jolly: In the literal way, we live in the sand, most of our places are in the sand. We wanted to live in the sand and to know what that brings to life. The house where I live has sand in it. We left the sand there in order to know what it brings to life. It brought something different because as we left those strips with the sand, we cannot approach furniture to the walls. We have a different way to configure furniture. That's a real thing. The second thing is that I have five children. They play a lot there. They like to play in it. Two things that come from the sand. The other thing is that during the first 20 years, we didn't touch the sand around the esperas. We left it just like that in order to see what we may build with the sand. Twenty years later, the sand was dirtier, absolutely dirty, because life, normal life, brings many things that make the sand become really dirty.

Purcell: Yes. The sand is a very good element in a wild situation. Fifteen inches from the house, moved by the wind, with the natural plants and all that, but immediately near the house, it dies. Twenty years later, we built some gardens in order to have the outside built because up to date, we haven't built a sand garden. That's it. In the metaphoric way, the sand poetically, the poet told us that meant "volver a no saber."

Volver A No Saber

Purcell: Yes. That is the point of view that doesn't mean ignorance. Volver a no saber, return to not knowing, means to see what you are going to do as anything, not as something already done or a born thing. That's the point of view of the sand. You see what we are looking at there. We want to live beside a sand it's always alive, not dead. That's a problem. That's what he was telling you. We have not managed yet to do that yet, but we're trying to.

" EVERYTHING ONE INVENTS IS TRUE,
YOU MAY BE PERFECTLY SURE OF THAT.
POETRY IS AS PRECISE AS GEOMETRY."
Gustave Flaubert

Epilogue

The dream of Ritoque's world famous school of architecture is to teach the students how to think for themselves - and then to turn those dreams and that form of independent thought into action, the actual building at the site of the Open City. They pride themselves on learning not from computer modeling but on "the realm of gesture and experience," in other words, mentorship, poetry, and hands on building.

The vision is ostensibly based on a work called the "Amereida." The centerpiece of their students' study at the Open City School of Architecture is a journey into the heart of South America. This is called the Amereida Traversa, a poem written by the Argentinan poet, Godofredo Iommi, in 1965. His epic is a meditation on the meaning of South America, is inspired by the French Surrealist poet Guillaume Apollinaire's conjoining of American with Aeneid, hence the "Amereida." In turn, the student's study is part of a quest for what is its own inheritance as those who live on a continent based half on Europe and half on native America.

For the students this symbolic annual journey reflects the quest to uncover what is real about the Latin America they both live in and are part of Ritoque itself is a Traversa, the school is embarked on a journey into its own unknown sea, enlightenment beckons down the road.

PC

CHAPTER 8

The Long Now

with

Stewart Brand

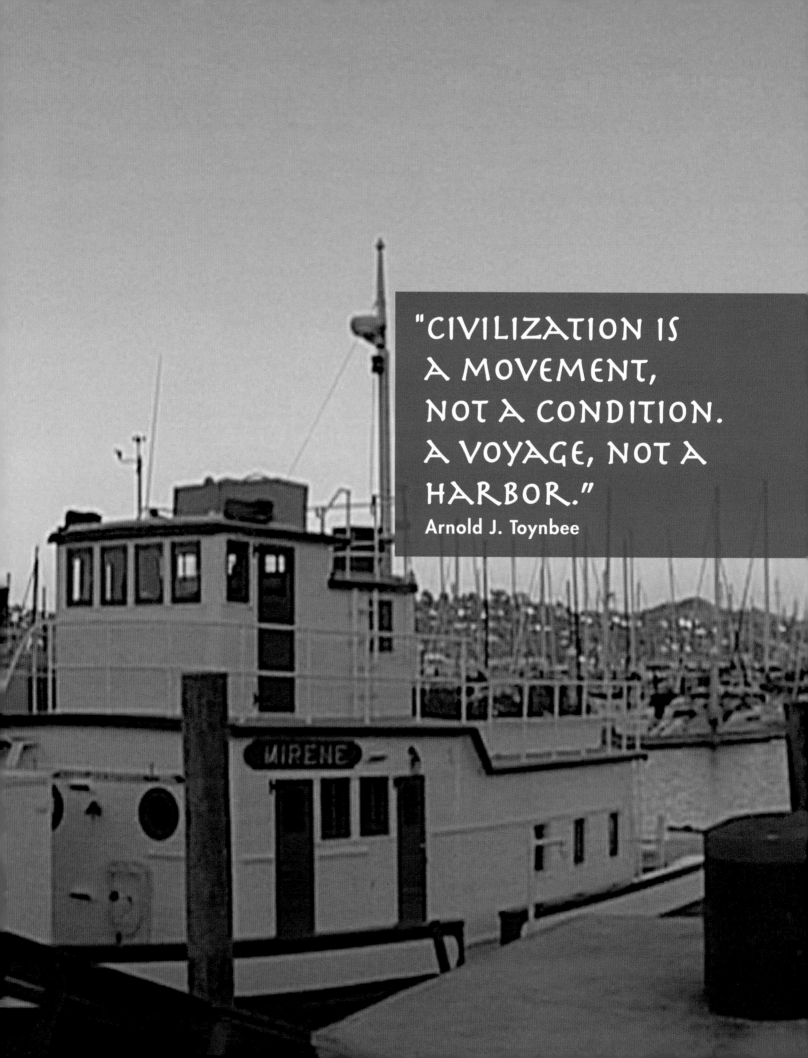

"CIVILIZATION IS A MOVEMENT, NOT A CONDITION. A VOYAGE, NOT A HARBOR."
Arnold J. Toynbee

As Stewart articulates in the film, we are just beginning to learn the skills of long-term thinking. Indeed, we have been terraforming the Earth for Millenniums; it is time to do it with an expanded sense of responsibility.

The Long Now organization that Brand co-founded postulates a 20,000 year frame of reference. We are now in the middle of the story. It is a liberating perspective to get beyond the never-ending news cycle, and learn to transmute it into an epic cycle.

As Thoreau wrote:

"Read the leaves of eternity,
not just current times."

Or as the English Bard William Blake once said:

"Eternity is in love with the
productions of time."

Stewart is one of the prime pathfinders to this brave new world of horizontal exchange of information. Thanks to his work and the Whole Earth Catalog network, the information monopolies have been splintered and fragmented into a multitude of pieces. Humpty Dumpty can't be put together again. All the Kings horses, and the all the King's men cannot change this new reality.

We now have this vast interactive world of personal media systems.

The Worlds of information and knowledge are instantlyavailable for weaving and re-weaving.

This is a fullfillment of a dream that goes back to Giulio Camillo and the Renaissance Memory Theater concept (see Chapter 2).

According to Stewart, part of the secret of learning to navigate this new world, is stacking polarities as a technique for stimulating new forms of creativity. Cybernetics combined with organic gardening; Artificial Intelligence mixed with biological design. Nomadics spliced with landscape architecture.

Along this line, his Orders of Civilization cross-section is an insightful tool for thinking in a comprehensive manner about the levels of pace and size in the working structure of a robust, adaptable civilization. As Stewart elegantly writes: The fast layers innovate, the slow layers stabilize. The whole combines learning with continuity.

There have been 24 Civilizations since recorded history.

They have risen and fallen in epochal time.

Accessing Stewart's perspective allows us to navigate the future with more intelligent lights.

As in the music of Bob Dylan, he draws us into his world, and we benefit from going on the voyage with him. Familiar, yet strange enough, that we want to know more.

CZ

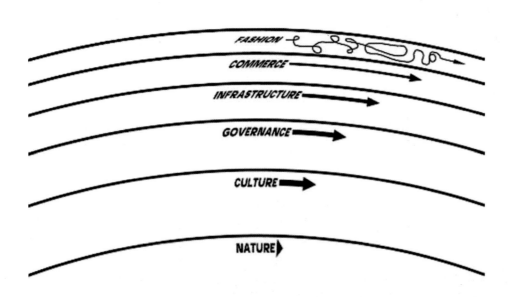

Chapter 8: Stewart Brand

Phil Cousineau: What is the relationship between communication and innovation?

Steward Brand: In my experience, innovation is usually credited to individuals, but as Brian Eno says, it's really not genius so much as scenius. It's a bunch of people who give each other a kind of encouragement and permission to create and be as good as each other, and better than each other and all of that. Anything that aids communication, and you see alot of this on the internet, facebook, and various kinds of crowd sourcing software, are giving people innovative environments that are pretty rich. You're getting various forms of what you might call "virtual cities." This is the sort of thing you used to go to cities physically. Some thought that once we can do it virtually, we won't go to physical cities anymore, but I suspect that's already proving to be exactly the opposite. When people in the countryside will get a taste of city life and virtual cities, pretty soon they will want the physical one. So the whole world is moving to town.

Cousineau: Do you have any thoughts on the recent idea of ephemeral cities? Is there anything to that idea?

Brand: I think a city is fundamentally ephemeral. It's ephemeral in terms of people moving around. It probably helps if it's somewhat ephemeral physically, that you are turning your buildings over fairly rapidly. If anything will completely paralyze New York, it may well be that they stop tearing down skyscrapers and putting up new ones they way they used to. There's various code things. There's various tourist things. There's various building preservation things, which I've promoted and still believe in, but it does kind of slow things down, maybe too much. I think the action is always going to be in places where the buildings feel like they're temporary, the occupancy feels like it's temporary. The whole deal about cities is they're about speed. They're about moving quickly, making contacts, doing stuff, doing businesses. If it fails, so what? Start another one. All this stuff is about urban speed, the hot New York minute. The city should accommodate that, reflect that, maybe give some solid ground. The streets are always have the same names, are in the same place from one century to the next. Everything else should probably stir around.

Cousineau: How does this collision between the desire to preserve tradition and memory versus the desire for change and innovation actually play out in urban life? They seem at odds with each other.

Brand: My sense is that most people's sense of memory is basically rural. People who move to some place like Lagos, Nigeria , they always have in mind the village where they were born. They go through a whole life in the city, but they want to be buried back in the village, if it's still there. The city is in constant flux. That's part of why they went there. That's why the only chance for many people to make money is when things are moving. My guess is as we move more and more toward being a city planet, more than half urban, the countryside will increasingly be the place where we place our sense of continuity with the past. It's where we will preserve the environment. You should keep the old cottage by the lake, wherever it might be, if that gives you a sense of grounding. So if the city is the figure of constant change, the ground then is the rural sense of continuity and memory. That may well mean that a lot of our cities become less obsessed with expressing memory physically. They'll have the museums, but I don't think you want too many monuments. This way we'll have the anniversaries that are looking back, but also freeing space for looking forward.

Cousineau: Are the two opposed then, the drive for urban design, urban renewal versus the emerging ethos of green design and eco-villages? Can they work side by side or are they opposed?

Brand: The history of utopias and dystopias are that utopias are always rural, and dystopias are always urban. Except for Poalo Soleri's arcologies, which are kind of an

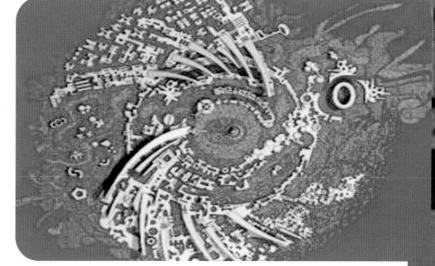

urban utopia, you never see it put in those terms, but my guess is that all those rural utopias tend toward dystopias pretty quickly. Some have done pretty well, but my generation of the '60's went out trying to start a bunch of intentional eco-villages. We lasted two or three years mostly, and then bounced back into town, either because we couldn't handle it. It was tough out there. We didn't make friends with the neighbors like we should have. Or there was no way to make money, which is the curse of rural life, or we just got bored, which is the real curse of rural life. It's going to be pretty tricky for these eco-villages to keep inventive people interested. It's fun for the first generation: "Wow! We're inventing a town. We're building Domes. We're having all this excitement. Let's start a family." But then what do you do for a second act? Typically the eco-villages, except for maybe Sri Auroribindo's Ashram in Pondicharry, India, which has had multiple generations go through it. I think most of them are good for about one generation.

Cousineau: Recently, you've made some distinctions between what you call "eco-romantics" and "eco-practicals." Could you help us sort that out?

Brand: I'm busy these days trying to figure out what the environmental frame of reference is. We now have climate changes, the major determinate of everything. It's useful to think about environmentalists in three sets: romantics, scientists, and engineers. First, romantics have been the long-term frame of reference for, basically, the Rousseauian version of the natural world, where the "natural person" becomes one with nature. It's sort of a political movement in solidarity with things like that. Second, the scientists just want to study nature. They like changing their mind, whereas romantics really don't like changing their mind once they've bought into a story. That's the way they want to live. The scientists like to argue; romantics try to keep people from arguing. Along comes now the third group, the engineers, who have this frame of reference which says: "Tell me what the problems are; then let's just fix them. Let's frame them in a way so they're tractable and so we can just go sort it all out."

The engineering approach is something that romantics obviously hate, like nuclear power, because they say nuclear energy is impossible. Engineers just look at it and say, "What are the problems here?" There are three or four major problems. Actually, if you take them apart and frame them in a way so they're solvable, you can solve them. Let's just go ahead and do that because it looks like a good thing to have in terms of not putting a lot of CO_2 into the atmosphere, which is the other problem we're trying to fix, the climate change in the atmosphere. Fixing the atmosphere is an idea that is really repellent to a lot of romantic environmentalists. They say whatever the atmosphere is now, is the way it ought to be, and we should just back off, so that it gets to keep being the way it is.

That frame of reference I'm comfortable with. I'm trained as a biologist. When things like genetic modification of foods and crops and various other things comes along, it looks to me like just good biology. It's called genetic engineering. Genetic engineering is a very tough pill to swallow for romantics, because they're pretty sure that Darwinian evolution didn't do that. As a biologist, I know that that's exactly what Darwinian evolution did and even more, microbial evolution, which is completely horizontal gene transfer. This is very much like what happens in cities. There is a lot of horizontal transfer of ideas, instead of a linear hierarchical approach to things, which is somewhat how we deal with sexual reproduction in evolution. I figure that by and by the Greens will catch on. If microbes

can do it that way and that's an inventive way to do things, we'll call it biomimickery, and we'll be okay with it.

Cousineau: I am fascinated by your reference to the Zuni mythology of continuous life, continuous change, continuous transformation. How can we make that a part of every day life?

Brand: I'm not sure that was mythology. That quote you referred to was by a Zuni anthropologist observing what happened to a Zuni Pueblo that she was familiar with, it was constantly changing. I think one of the reasons Zuni is the most intact culture in the Southwest, along with Navajos, is precisely because of this point--they are so constantly changing. A lot of the other Pueblos, which are basically little eco-villages, got kind of stuck. That wasn't because they were just abiding by tradition, which the Zuni's have absolutely intact, but because they were stuck economically or intellectually, or maybe spiritually. I don't know. I do know the shalako dance and the blue corn dance, and all these rituals and ceremonies, are really alive and well in the Zunis. They are famous

among anthropologists. If you can take a Zuni, parachute them anywhere in the world, he'll hit the ground, learn the local language, get a job, and be back at Zuni in time for the Blue Corn Festival. They're competent in the world. Maybe that's what urbanity really is: competence in the world so that you can go anywhere and prevail. Just figure out a way to learn the language, learn the economy, fit into it, and then make things go your way. That's what urban people do.

Cousineau: Are they able to do this because they have practiced for a millennia what you call The Art of the Long View? As opposed to the long body? Is there a correlation here?

Brand: Mohawks are the ones who figured out how to be the high steel workers in New York. I guess they brought a tribal sense of pride and bravery to that job, which typically, Native Americans also bring to military service as warriors. Having a sense of who you are can be a great confidence builder. It can probably also get in your way in terms of not getting off your ass. Maybe that's the paradox that we're talking about here. A study I haven't seen done, that would be interesting to do, would be to compare people who left the village to go to a big city with those people who stayed behind. Who are they? What's different about them? How did their lives turn out? How do relations between them, if any, continue over time? As far as I know, that study hasn't been done. We would learn a lot. Some of it is classic, early adopter's behavior. A new tool comes along, there's some

people who want to go play with it. Folks living in a village see a lot of stuff coming to and from the city.

They have to swim upstream to where all that innovation is coming from. Whereas, other folks are saying, "Write if you get work." They do get work often, and then they do write. Then other people follow that path. So you get the later adopters. Some bounce off the city, and who's that? What happened there? I don't really know. I know people who stayed in Rockford, Illinois, where I grew up. I don't know them very well anymore. Others, who left, hit the west coast, bounced right off it, and went back to Illinois. They knew thoroughly how to do Rockford, but not so thoroughly how to do San Francisco. In any culture, you want some people who are doing Rockford, and some people who are doing

San Francisco. That combination gives you a flywheel; it gives you a range of activities. It gives you a place to fall back to if the plague hits the big cities. More and more people don't know how to do small towns anymore. You've got to have someone out there who can still do that.

Cousineau: What you deem "the Art of the Long Now" is a poetic way of thinking about our responsibility toward future generations. Is there a way to practice the art of the long now? Can this way of thinking about time become part of our everyday life, what you've called "eco-pragmatism?"

Brand: I think where the idea I'm exploring of eco-pragmatism meets long-term thinking, is in the whole concept of options, of keeping options open so we don't let species go extinct. You don't let your climate go completely chaotic, because that's a situation where options are now narrower for people in the future. The time frame's a pretty long one. Species coming and going is a long time frame. Climate coming and going is a long time frame. Thinking about the future in these terms is not about figuring out the right plan for the future and making it happen, it's figuring out what options that now exist that have been preserved for us by our ancestors. We want to keep those options intact for our descendants. Our gift to them is to add some more options that maybe they didn't have before, and so we have more strange things they can try. They have more resilience built into the full range of activities going on in their civilization. Anything that narrows options in that view is a problem. Anything that opens up options is potentially good. In ecological terms, something like genetic modification might not look acceptable, but I think pragmatically it is.

Cousineau: Your closing statement in your book, Clock of the Long Now is very compelling. It rings like a challenge to our generation. It's the line about feeling and the responsibility that

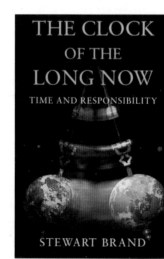

THE CLOCK
OF THE
LONG NOW
TIME AND RESPONSIBILITY

STEWART BRAND

you have to your children and grandchildren.

Brand: I think it was Rosabeth Moss Kanter who was talking about what social situations make people comfortable thinking long term. One situation is a sense of that there are pretty reliable rules that everybody can have in mind and are somewhat accountable in relation to. There is also the sense that the past generations are present and the future generations are present, in terms of how you're taking care of kids, in terms of education, in terms of the way you're teaching science. In terms of opening up whole new kinds of employment and useful things to do in the world, and so on. That what you're looking for is enough comfort in the world that people will try new stuff, and I suppose enough discomfort in the world that they won't just sit there. That combination is especially rich in cities, and maybe that's one of the attractions.

I think we've just begun to think, to learn how to think long term. Science is giving us more and more knowledge about how the world has actually gone over the past centuries, the millennia, millions of years. Some of the deep, formerly mysterious forces, that we're coming to understand, such as climate, that have these very long time frames, and that we have impact on. For good or ill, it's as if we were "terraforming" Earth, as if it was a planet that we'd just come to, and we're doing it very badly. Badly enough at present, that we need to worry about it. We don't have a choice in not terraforming Earth anymore. Earth is now a city planet, a really urban planet. The planet has got so much human stuff going on that the planet is now an artifact of human activities. Marshall McLuhan was right about that.

If that's the case, then we have some responsibility to not terraform badly. If we do bad things on the planet, it feeds back on us immediately. For instance, you can't breathe in Beijing these days. So our actions feedback in terrible ways, in karmic ways over decades and centuries. When you bear that in mind, it starts to give you a frame of reference, a kind of permission to go ahead and fund the things that have this kind of infrastructural frame of reference. Saying "this is something we're doing for the decades," or "this is something we're doing for the centuries. That's why we're doing it." Yes it's expensive in present terms, but it's a bargain in terms of decades and centuries.

Cousineau: The legendary Beat poet Gary Snyder writes about how important it is to keep alive the sense of wild in us. Does that phrase "wild thinking" mean anything to you?

Brand: There's a book called Tending the Wild, by a woman in Davis, California. Basically, it is about how California was a garden run by the 26 tribal groups and language groups that lived here

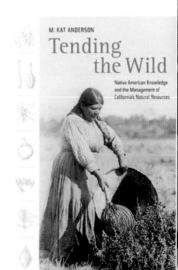

before whites showed up. The whole bloody state was farmed, burned, gardened. The California tribes were growing things on purpose, and defending things on purpose. It was a rich landscape, because they made it a rich landscape. She was a white woman who went with some Indians up into the Trinity Alps, a wild place in the north of California, which is well protected now as a state park. These Indians looked at it and said, "Look at this place. It's a mess. It's just a wilderness." Meaning it no longer had humans in it. It was no longer functioning in relationship to humans. It had been dehumanized and, as far as they were concerned, it was just a waste.

What we think of as the wild, has been very, very minutely tended for tens of thousands of years that humans have been in North America, and the many tens of thousands of years they've been elsewhere. We're starting to find the Amazon Basin was this huge agricultural expanse with villages and cities every so often. What is wilderness now, was a stone civilization back when. Those folks died out with the European plague that came with the conquistadores. In the jungle, it's hard to see what was left, because they didn't build with stone; there's no stone there.

I think the "wild" is a kind of romanticized state of mind. It's absolutely true what Thoreau said: "In the wildness is the preservation of the world." How long was he in his shack? About a year and a half. It wasn't that far from town. Wilderness and the rural landscape is increasingly a place that we will be in the future, not living in so much as visiting. We'll be visiting it with this voluntary engagement with great big systems that we basically don't control. That's always wholesome.

Cousineau: Why then did you choose to put the Clock of the Long Now in the wilderness? Are you nudging them along in the direction of a pilgrimage so it's a conscientious journey to see this?

Brand: The idea of the Clock of the Long Now, a 10,000-year clock, really has two forms. There's the mountain clock and a city clock. The city clock ideally would be in some busy city. Singapore was almost it. Jerusalem was almost it. Who knows who will eventually get a serious city clock. It'll be a point of long-term reference that probably won't really last more than a few centuries, because cities turn over. They get bombed, various things happen. Water rises, because they're on the coast. Things that are in a countryside and things that are underground last a long time. The mountain clock is planned for serious country in eastern Nevada, and in a very strong mountain made out of dense Permian limestone. Anything that's installed in there is going to last a long time.

The idea is that to do the pilgrimage to the clock, you will need to

> " I NEVER SAW A WILD THING SORRY FOR ITSELF. A SMALL BIRD WILL DROP FROZEN DEAD FROM A BOUGH WITHOUT EVER HAVING FELT SORRY FOR ITSELF."
> D.H. Lawrence

walk across this timeless countryside, climb up this timeless mountain, disappear into it, experience the clock, come out the top among bristlecone pines, some of them are 4,000 and 5,000 years old and still alive. Look out at 100 miles of pretty wild Nevada, which is the definitive long view. This is not a metaphor: it's the real thing. You've just had an experience, and now you've got to get yourself down the mountain. In a sense, we are building around an experience which is out of contemporary time. To ensure the experience of the long view, we're trying to do is preserve the valley that you see from the mountains, a 500-square-mile valley called Spring Valley. It's in pretty good shape now. We're busy trying to further preserve it, restore it, protect it, make it part of the National Park, and be sure that when somebody goes up the mountain, they experience the clock and are able to look out at the world. The world out there has a timeless quality that they can see and sense that it will retain that timeless quality. What you then get from the clock and from the landscape around it is a feeling that you've got a telescope that's looking right through the centuries. Things are going to change like mad, but probably this clock is going to keep ticking, and that landscape is just going to keep being sagebrush county.

Cousineau: What's the relationship between the deep time that's evoked by this vision, and deep design? Is it partly a response to planned obsolescence?

Brand: My problem with the idea of planned obsolescence is the planned part. Voluntary obsolescence is just fine. In a sense, it's the nature of temporary buildings that you see on the parts of campus that were built during the war. These are temporary buildings that all the cool new stuff goes on in, and there's rapid, rapid turnover. The amenities are not so great. It's really hot in the summer, cold in the winter, and nobody cares what you do in there. That's, in a way, what Buckminster Fuller described as an "outlaw area." It's an area which has fewer rules and regulations, because basically nobody cares. That's where you can do lots of innovation, try lots of things, because nobody cares if you fail. That's where young people can experiment, because they'll put up with anything. That's part of the teaching, learning, trying stuff process. I think any city that loses its outlaw area, loses its bohemia or its artist community, is probably going to be culturally impoverished after a while .

Another thing that would be fun to do is to create "maps over time" of where the artist community is moving in various towns like London, or San Francisco, or New York. They move. They keep moving. The place grows so impoverished that nobody will live there. It's not even worth burning the buildings down for insurance anymore. Artists move in because it costs nothing to live there and they don't have any money. They start getting creative. Pretty soon there's some nice places to eat. Pretty soon there's some galleries, and the rents go up, and other people start living there. Soon after you get some more amenities and it gets gentrified, by which time, the artists have moved on to the next part of town that has gone to hell, and then they start trying to save that one.

In San Francisco, the gay community basically moved into these falling-apart old Victorians, and completely spruced them up. They were double-income couples, with no kids. They had plenty of money to paint every little nook and cranny of these Victorian exteriors that had been viewed with great disdain by everybody who cared about cities and design, the so-called experts who said, "those terrible Victorians." The gays just came along and said, "What do you mean terrible? These are seriously fun buildings. They're completely livable-look!" They decorated San Francisco basically, inside and out, and saved the town.

Cousineau: You've used the phrase "city laboratories" in your books and lectures, which makes me wonder what you think about the phenomenon of "dying cities?"

Brand: The world is littered with ruins of dead cities, which suggests to me that while cities are the longest-lived human institutions we have. That doesn't mean that all of them are the longest lived institutions we have. Some cities really do die. Famously, capital cities die, if you get a new emperor in China, who says, "We're going to have the seat of government over here instead of over there. That was the old world and I'm the new world, and we're going over here." In cases like that the old place just turns into sand. Then you have places like New Orleans or where climate change makes it basically impossible to live there and people just stop living there, and that's that.

If cities that were tied to a particular industry in a really big way, and then that industry goes away, as industries will do, and they're not able to move to the next platform, then you have a kind of a slow motion gold rush town, a kind of mining boomtown: "Wow! There's a whole town and they got 25 bars and 2 churches, and people raising their kids." But 25 years later, there's no metal left in the ground and everybody's gone. It's a ghost town. So you have fast motion and slow motion ghost towns, and that's probably fine.

In the case of Detroit, maybe the thing to do is to declare it is dead from here on, though there's some interesting buildings. We'll keep them just the way Henry Ford did when he brought those old heritage buildings: Edison's Laboratory, Wright Brothers bicycle shop, etc. in from all over the country and created Greenfield Village, in Dearborn. Maybe the whole city of downtown Detroit, maybe the whole urban area of Detroit, is going to be like this. We'll just pour acrylic all over it and this wonderful place that you can see is absolutely stuck in the amber like a mosquito from millennia before. We will tell our children, "That's what it was like back in the 1950s. They built cars." And when children ask, "What are cars, Daddy?" We'll say, "See, there's one right there." Maybe that's the thing to do with dead old cities, is find ways to let them die. It's okay. Other towns are doing fine, and you don't have to sustain all of them. I imagine this is very hard to sell (laughs) in a democratic society, but it may not be a question of selling, it just happens.

Cousineau: Is it possible for a city to reinvent itself today?

Brand: I think a bay city can always reinvent itself, unless it's New Orleans and the water rises, and hurricanes come. Cities that are on consequential edges, the edges of mountains, like Denver, have this quality of reinventing themselves. At the eastern end of the Mediterranean, you find Jerusalem, which was a very consequential city back when, it is also a very consequential city right now because there's has always been so much trade activity, cultural traffic, moving through it.

Same thing with Alexandria. Alexandria turns out actually was a town before Alexander decreed that there will be a city there. It had been a trading outpost, and then he tranformed into a larger one, and then a cultural city and all the rest of it. That city died, but the town goes on for other good reasons.

Cousineau: Do you agree with Sir Peter Hall, cities are supposed to be the civilizing force?

Brand: I'm pretty sure that the etymology tells us that cities and civilization are the same word. Citizen and civic come from the Latin civitas, which I think gives us city and civilization. Historians pretty much say now, when we're talking about civilization, what we're talking about is what happens in cities.

Cousineau: You've written that some of the worst destruction in urban life comes from making decisions too quickly, change too fast, and that you are on the side of slow change.

Brand: I think there are parts of cities that you do want to change relatively slowly. Libraries, museums, universities, maybe the town hall, but not necessarily some of the deep infrastructure. Certainly the geography, if you've got hills, don't flatten them. Get used to them. If you've got a river, don't try to pretend it isn't there. Figure out how to celebrate it. Once you've figured out the things you want to keep, part of the reason you've done that is that it then gives you a frame on which to make a whole lot of things change, as rapidly as they want to change. Then out of the same sense of responsibility that helped you to protect the river, can assist you to get out of the way of things that want to change rapidly, like business, and not burden them with a whole lot of regulations. Likewise with an artist community that is taking some chances

and behaving strangely. It's at least amusing, and maybe profoundly creative. You don't know until later, but let it happen. Letting that high flux stuff go on the same time you're protecting the river, is part of running a city well.

Zelov: Can scenario planning apply to the future of cities?

Brand: If you were going to do scenario planning for cities or planning how cities might go in the future, what you need to look for are the driving forces. Driving forces are things like economics. If people can make money in cities, they'll make the journey to cities in order to make money. If they can't, they won't. Especially, if they have a really tough time making money out in the countryside. They will leave the countryside to go to where they can make money, which is in the cities, which may or may not be in their own country. It may well be in a whole different part of the world. They'll go to the cities there, and they'll put up with a lot. Economics is a big part of a driving force that could go one way or another. One thing you would look for is things that would reverse a trend, the trend of more and more concentration in cities, a million people in a square mile basically. If you have certain kinds of pandemics, density of humans, color, whatever it might be, you can't just send everybody out of town fast in order to save their life. We could well have an avian flu type pandemic that takes off, that goes from airport to airport, hospital to hospital, which would make it a serious problem that would force people to flee. If it's a lingering disease, then you'll have a completely different urban environment for a good while. If it's a thing which is over in a couple of years, people will come right back; but when they come back it will be different, like London was after the Great Fire of 1666. Likewise, wars have a tendency to erase some cities. Baghdad is going to have to be reinvented pretty soon. Many European cities and much of London, was reinvented after the second World War. Some of them put it back right exactly the way it was, not giving

the war any honor at all, and just pretend it never happened. Others city planners after the war said, "No. while we're at it, let's just try some other stuff."

Big things can happen. There are peculiarities going on with demographics. Demographics is the thing that futurists most rely on, because it is the closest thing you get to a really faithful sense of what's going to happen in the future. For example, the demographic right now is that the global north is getting steadily older and not making that many babies. Its population is going down. The global south is still making babies, not as many as they used to, but the grand result is that they're making these huge brand new cities, megalopolises of enormous scale, tens of millions, up over 20 million in some cases, such as Mexico City. The urban innovation is all going to be in the global south for the next half century. I suppose we'll have urban conservatism because of folks not wanting to change their ways that much and not having young people who are going to push them. We may well have a relatively static north and a highly dynamic South. That could be good for everybody, or if they choose to fight each other, it could be pretty vicious for everybody, because you've got a lot of young male soldiers in the South, and a lot of people are not going to serve in the military anymore in the North. How that plays out could go several different scenaric paths. So one of the key scenarios you want to think about is the dynamic between northern cities and southern cities over the next few decades.

Cousineau: Will we recognize our cities 500 years, 1,000 years in the future? Do you anticipate so much change that they would be unrecognizable, or would we be able to recognize the core that hasn't changed?

Brand: If a city were going to be recognizable 500 years from now, it would have to be because somebody had the intention and maintained the intention that it was going to be recognizable. In the absence of that, cities are so constantly metamorphic that I think in their own terms, they would be, to us, unrecognizable. Now, if it's the case that people actually do get the ability to live 100 years, 200 years, 300 years, 400 years, 500 years, and there are some people around 500 years from now who are alive now, that may put enough conservatism in the culture and in the continuity that those people-who'd presumably be very powerful and very rich, assuming that they've got all of their marbles and capabilities, and the young bodies that they've implanted or whatever. They would want that continuity because old people like things sort of somewhat recognizable and are in pain when they're not recognizable. One scenario would go toward cities that would be recognizable, if we have people living that long. Another scenario would say without that, without some intention to maintain a visual experienceable continuity, there wouldn't be one, they might have a few monements, the Temple, the rock, the wailing wall, and things like that in Jerusalem. Whether a city like New York would last 500 more years, I don't know, water levels change, and alot would change with that, they could put dikes around it. Is it going to going to become some kind of Amsterdam? I don't know. Or you could have some cities specialize in continuity and other specialize in discontinuity. Fez is pretty recogizable now as a working medieval city in doing the same stuff it did when it was the middle ages. You go down in the souks and you can buy and sell, and see people making things partly with their toes, the way they used to; that is still valuable to people. At this scale, the little shop on the street scale, may continue. But I would imagine that Los Angeles would not try to be recognizable. Why would it bother?

> "HUMANKIND HAS NOT WOVEN THE WEB OF LIFE.
> WE ARE BUT ONE THREAD WITHIN IT.
> WHATEVER WE DO TO THE WEB, WE DO TO OURSELVES.
> ALL THINGS ARE BOUND TOGETHER.
> ALL THINGS CONNECT."
> Chief Seattle, 1854

Cousineau: In Jared Diamond's book, Collapse, he describes himself as a cautious optimist. Do you think that's a reasonable position for the future?

Brand: I think a cautious optimist, like Jared Diamond, is being a responsible professor who's got to look pretty good over decades, in terms of what he says. God knows I honor Jared Diamond extremely highly. He's a first-rate scientist, a first-rate writer, and he's changed how we think about history and many other things. I kind of like incautious optimists because they're the ones who will try stuff rather than just expect other people to try stuff. A cautious optimist assumes nice things will go on. Somebody will make things happen. An incautious optimist says, "Actually, that's my job, to make things happen." A culture needs a fair number of those. Just one or two is not enough. I think one of the things cities can do for civilization is attract a bunch of those incautious optimists together into critical masses where they set each other loose in a metaphoric fashion.

> " THE TROUBLE WITH
> OUR TIMES IS THAT
> THE FUTURE IS NOT
> WHAT IT USED TO BE."
> Paul Valery

Cousineau: Since the days of <u>Co-Evolutionary Quarterly</u>, you have been asscociated with a story that took place at The New College at Oxford. Can you indulge us one more time and describe to us how it served you as a parable, a teaching story, for urban planners, even for kids who are learning about Sustainable Design.

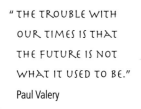

Brand: The story of the oak beams of New College Oxford I got from Gregory Bateson, and he got it from somebody who'd actually been there at the New College. It's become a twice-told story. New College was called New because it was built relatively late in the set of colleges at Oxford in the 14th century. Like most other colleges at the time, they built a great big college hall, and it had a 30-foot or so cross joist inside, very high, and big beautiful oak beams up there. In the 19th century, as Gregory said, a busy entomologist climbed up to examine the beams and discovered that the beams were getting seriously weak because they were full of beetles. Then the college fathers got together and said, "Oh my God, what are we going to do? Where are we going to find trees of that caliber anymore?" They called in the college forester, who hadn't been anywhere near the college in years because he was out managing the college lands hither and yon. They said, "We're in trouble. We need big oak trees." He tugged his forelock and said, "Well, sirs, we was wondering when you'd be asking." It turns out that hundreds of years before, oaks had been planted and protected for many centuries, because they knew then that oak

145

beams eventually do get beetley and would need to be replaced. The College had planted oak trees so that they would be fully grown when that need came up.

As Gregory says, "That's the way to run a culture."

Cousineau: Almost without exception when you've told this story in public, a single question comes up again and again.

Brand: Have they planted new trees? I went to New College Oxford with the BBC, and we shot the story there. There is a woman who said she was a college historian, who kept saying, "No, no, no. That never happened. No, no, no. That's not true." I gave her some documents that I'd found, actually it did happen. I said, "Have you guys planted trees for the next time these things get beetley, because they're going to." Not a subject they're ready to talk about at all. Regardless, I think by the next time around, when Oxford needs to replace the oak beams again, we'll have some genetically modified oaks that you can grow in about five years, and so they'll be fine.

Cousineau: Is there anything there in the Oxford story that you can talk about as a parable?

Brand: The Oak Beams in New College Oxford has become sort of shorthand as a way to refer to thinking ahead that is basically infrastructural. Great big beams. This is not the style of the building. This is not what kind of teaching is going to go on in the building. This is just the thing that keeps the rain out, and lets people all dine together in this one big space, which you assume will continue to be a good idea with the professor at the high table, and all the rest of that story. Then, I think particularly in North America with our veneration of our somewhat romanticized British ancestry, all you have to do is say Oxford and people just get all melty. Ooh! 14th century. Ooh! continuity from that. That's permission to, because then one is so comfortable engaging those six centuries that have just been embraced in one idea, looking back. People looking forward from there; then you can make the jump of, "Okay, what would we do if we were looking forward six centuries from now? What are the oak beams in our world that we would like to be planting acorns and protecting their growth?" That's a really open question because it's probably not oaks, but what is it?

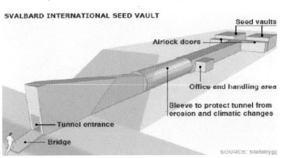

SVALBARD INTERNATIONAL SEED VAULT
Seed vaults
Airlock doors
Office and handling area
Sleeve to protect tunnel from erosion and climatic changes
Tunnel entrance
Bridge
SOURCE: statsbyge

Cousineau: Can you tell us about the implication of that story for us today? How that serves as a parable for us not taking care of the "Seventh Generation," as the Native American Elders say.

Brand: I think there's a tremendous amount of romanticism of North American Indians, including by Indians. The seventh generation thing has become so common that I thought, "You know, it'd be really nice to track this down." Everything that I looked up led back to the Iroquois League Document, and the guy who invented the Iroquois League. The Iroquois League is this amazing Robert's Rules of Order for the way they ran their sort of military alliance. It has some tough stuff in it, like if one of the representatives to the council got too far out of order, the chairman of the council could give permission to the other council members to beat that person to death. That's serious Robert's Rules of Order. It has that kind of stuff in there, but it also has some kind of classic Indian jokey stuff in it. One of the things it says is, that the kinds of representatives you're going to want from each of these tribes to come to these councils have got to be pretty thick-skinned, because they're going to catch all kinds of flak from everybody. They're going to catch it from each other. They're going to catch it from their own tribe, because they're going to be coming back with things the tribe doesn't want to do. They've got to have a skin as thick as the bark of a tree that's seven generations old. That's it. That's the seven generation story. It's an Indian joke. Now it's true that a page or two later, they're saying part of the responsibilities of a council member is to bear future generations in mind and bear the past in mind. That's part of what we mean by responsibility. There's enough about seven generations there. I would want to look at the Black Elk stuff because Neihardt was always a romanticist, to put it mildly. It's a great story. The Iroquois League was on the way to becoming like one of the central American empires. It would've been if the Europeans, and our diseases, had not come along. My first wife's a Chippewa and Algonquin. Her Algonquins were pushed west basically by the success of the Iroquois League. The Algonquins then pushed the Dakota, the Sioux, out of the woods into the prairie, and they all became horse Indians when the horses arrived. Up until then, they were just the poor bastards who couldn't live in the woods anymore because the Chippewas had pushed them out. They'd been pushed by the Iroquois because of that guide, who invented a very powerful alliance system that, I think there's some plausible argument that the people who wrote the U.S. Constitution were aware of and respectful of. They were studying Venice. They were studying Rome. To some extent, they were studying Greece, but not so much. They were studying everybody that had innovative forms of governance, and the Iroquois was one of them.

Cousineau: Can you talk about the orders of civilization model you developed?

147

Brand: First you have the order of Nature. Then you get some slower orders like infrastructures, more the multi-decade thing, get on down to the pretty seriously slower stuff like governance. Governments come and go, but a good governmental situation won't change quickly. How you do your democracy or how you do your royalty or whatever it might be. I think Churchill was right that keeping the royal family in England was a useful thing to do because a royal family thinks in generations. That's one of the things you would like to have in a government. We don't have it in the U.S. We've got to build a 10,000-year clock instead. Then you get down to slower stuff like culture. This is language. It's religion. It is deeply conservative. It's not going to change quickly. If you force it to change quickly, bad things happen. Even slower than that is basically natural cycles. Forests come and go. Water levels that go up and down. Rivers that wave around. That's not only deeply slow, but deeply powerful. Part of the idea of this approach, thinking about a civilization, is that while we tend to put all of our attention

on the rapidly changing stuff, that's what we're reading about in the daily newspaper, looking at on television, studying on the internet, blogging about, the slow stuff has all the power. That's what's setting the rules. That's what's forming the continuity. That's what's deciding which of all these things that are flipping on by, in commerce and fashion, are worth actually keeping. Some fads become permanent, and that is decided by the libraries, and the museums, and the colleges, and the governance, and all that slow-moving, slow-grinding, fine-grinding stuff. Where do cities fit in that? My sense is that, the way I do this graphically is I take this sort of equal shape of those different layers and then Photoshop it so that fashion and commerce are big, and nature and culture are small, and everything moves toward the rapidly moving stuff. The role of cities is to be a place where all that rapid stuff can move as rapidly as they want, and absorb shocks to the culture, and try stuff, and try and fail, try and fail, try and succeed. Then the success is kept by the whole culture. Cities' role is to take all those base layers and leave none out, and have no disrespect between the layers, but basically focus on the fast moving stuff. Give it unleashed freedom to move really, really quickly, and completely honor and maintain the slow stuff, but it's not the main event, the way it may be in the capital or in the whole countryside of a particular civilization. That's how cities fit into my cross-section of civilization.

Cousineau: Do you appreciate Bucky's idea that the true change, the true creativity, comes from the design outlaw, those who are on the periphery rather

than in the institutions, in the center?

Brand: Buckminster Fuller's idea of the outlaw area and the outlaw designer is somewhat a romantic one, and sort of appealed to us young folks in the '60's, and we loved that. If we couldn't be anything else, we could be outlaws and outlaw designers. That was fun and we were. Bucky had in mind, I think, basically the oceans. He was always a pretty, he had a seafaring mind, and that was…The oceans are pretty outlaw now, but I don't think they're as creative for a civilization as the outlaw areas in the squatter cities and the slums of the world, which is where people aren't paying taxes. They don't have title to the property. They're not part of the formal economy. They're just getting by and creating whatever they need to function. They'll take cell phones and turn them into little automated cash machines just by being innovative. That's happening in the poor part of town and in the relatively unstructured, unregulated part of town. In that sense, Bucky's notion of the outlaw designer really does play out. It's not the only place that design happens. Now that I'm no longer a young person, I'm paying attention to other places where design happens. Some of it is on purpose and by people who are paid to do it.

Cousineau: What are you working on now?

Brand: We have this organization called the Long Now Foundation, which is fostering a long-term responsibility. Long Now, what's that? The idea comes from Brian Eno and Peter Schwartz. Brian Eno had the notion that we get into trouble when our now is kind of a short now, since last week, this week, and next week. That's all we take responsibility for. Peter Schwartz said, "Well, civilization's been going on for 10,000 years, basically since the northern ice receded. We started having agriculture and cities. Civilization's story begins 10,000 years ago. A nice round number." To be symmetrical, say the next 10,000 years is an equal time frame and assume that we're in the middle of civilization's story. We're not at the beginning of a new civilization. We're not at the end of he civilization. We're in the middle of the story. That's a normal thing to do. How are we doing so far? You check on the story that we've got up until now. What have we got in mind or what do we want to keep possibilities open for the next 10,000 years? The Long Now is 20,000 years long and why not hold it in mind, though we hold last week, this week, and next week in mind, as something that we bear a relation to personally. We have responsibility for what goes on. We can schedule stuff over the next week. We can schedule it over the next few thousand years. When are we going to go to Mars? Well, that's not a decision that necessarily you make in one year for something, you're going to do the next year. When are we going to make sure that nobody's hungry in the world? You can decide all you want, but you're not going to make that happen in a year. You've got to figure that's a half a century project, but it's worth taking on so we'll do it. All you're getting from this long time frame is a sense of responsibility, sure, but also a freedom not to have to accomplish everything right now, not to have to accomplish everything in one's own lifetime.

One of the things the Long Now gets you to do, the ability to break through the barrier of your lifetime, and take things that happen before you were born very seriously. As the truism says, much was decided before you were born and much will be decided after we die, but we bear relation to that. We are part of that long decision making process and there's a comfort in it of

the kind that people get from long-lived institutions. I've been in the military. People who stay in the military for their entire career, have a sense of the long gray line of they can sing about the shores of Tripoli, and that feels personal to them. They feel that that institution is going to carry on long past their career and their life, and they have some responsibilities to that. People who have a strong religious church affiliation, have the same kind of sense. Some people can feel that about a city. Some can feel it about a nation. That's, I think, good stuff to have. These institutional, long time frame, sets of references, that's the oak beams in New College Oxford. That's assuming that there is going to be a New College Oxford five centuries from now, and what do we do now to make sure that it's in good order?

Cousineau: Do you have any final thoughts?

Brand: No. They're all final.

Creating Gaviotas

with

Paolo Lugari

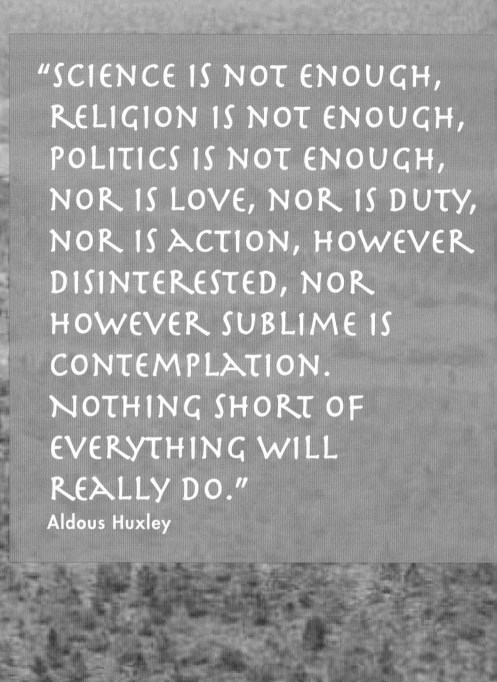

"SCIENCE IS NOT ENOUGH, RELIGION IS NOT ENOUGH, POLITICS IS NOT ENOUGH, NOR IS LOVE, NOR IS DUTY, NOR IS ACTION, HOWEVER DISINTERESTED, NOR HOWEVER SUBLIME IS CONTEMPLATION. NOTHING SHORT OF EVERYTHING WILL REALLY DO."

Aldous Huxley

Gaviotas is a glowing example that sustainable settlements can be forged in extreme conditions. Indeed, a big part of its beauty stems from the in-extremis aspect of the endeavor.

To our over-urbanized frame of reference, Gaviotas may seem like a quixotic quest, similar to finding the Northwest Passage. However, it is a passage that our petroleum imbued civilization as we know it must find a way to navigate toward.

Paolo Lugari thunders forth with an inventive mindset that discloses the way for a new world to be brought forth. He is contunually working with the creativity of the original chaos, which subsequently permits us to form a Cosmos. As he states in our interview: Gaviotas is on a "permanent quest for temporary truth."

Transforming the crisis of imagination in our cities is crucial to making our cities more livable. Lugari calls for a new symbiosis between progress and human happiness. A crucial part of which is re-appreciating that the gift of creativity as the prime gift of being in the human form.

In the battle against the baldness of the Earth and the looming issues of Climate Change, Lugari has proposed a new type of City that has a Bio-Remediational aspiration. Making a comparison with John F. Kennedy's call to put a man on the moon in ten years, he appeals to the transcendent capacity of the human spirit.

Lugari's list of names for this mission to re-invent the City include:

- **The City of the New Millenium**
- **The Re-Enchanted City**
- **The Reborn City**
- **Felicitas**
- **The Sensible City**
- **The Illuminated City**

- **The Musical Bio-City**
- **Tropicalus**
- **Vitalitas**

Bring forth the Dance of Shiva. Destroy the insipid, cretinous, and unregenerative.

Make space for more artistry. Send the dogs of dogma back to the lands of the priestcraft. Make new arrangements of the apertures in which we see the future.

As Emerson once said:

> *"People only see what they are prepared to see."*

Let's re-enchant the route to a better metropolis.

Lugari connects the quest for a sustainable culture, to the search for happiness.

Since humans are apparently built to pursue happiness, are we then destined to create a more sustainable world? Can Biological Capitalism emerge out of the conceptual wilderness into a new foyer opening the gates to a augmented form of 21st Century contemporary life?

The quest to evolve the status quo is timeless. As the great comparative mythologist Joseph Campbell further articulates:

> *"... the mythological hero is the champion not of things become but of things becoming; the dragon to be slain by him is precisely the monster of the status quo: Holdfast, the keeper of the past. From obscurity the hero emerges, but the enemy is great and conspicuous in the seat of power; he is enemy, dragon, tyrant, because he turns to his own advantage the authority of his position. He is Holdfast not because he keeps the past but because he keeps."*

Chapter 9: Paolo Lugari

Christopher Zelov: Can you describe your philosophy of development at Gaviotas?

Paolo Lugari: In Gaviotas, we are on a permanent quest for temporary truths. Within this context, I would like to point out that for us development has to be seen within a systemic context, so that it has as an axis, a sustainability, where everything is within everything.

Therefore, Gaviotas is a "holarchy", which is an invented word of ours, which means "everything is in it." For us, a holarchy is like an equilateral triangle. On one side is nature, on the other side is technology, and on the baseline, the human race and all other species. This means that we have to be feasible economically, culturally and environmentally, simultaneously. For us, Gaviotas is a university in this sense.

Therefore, Gaviotas is for us a kind of university, which means the diversity within the unity. Quite opposite to what happens with a university in the West, which often tends to standardize knowledge, negating diversity, and close in on its students. This way of seeing development, which is not a school because it's not a finished body of thought, can be translated to the growth and development of cities in particular.

In the tropics, we have examples of early settlements that stand out. There were two sites in Mesoamerica with organic human settlements, cities of more than 300,000 inhabitants, at a time when the main European cities were just a group of farms. Mesoamerica was a place where a tropical civilization came from. After all, the word civilization is related to the word city.

Two hundred years ago, when the United States declared independence, the regions and cities of Latin America were much more advanced than the North American cities. We forgot about the tropics and we started to think in a manner of four seasons. In the tropics, nature works in a continuous way. In the north, it works by seasons, by stages.

> "THE MARCH OF INVENTION HAS CLOTHED MANKIND WITH POWERS OF WHICH A CENTURY AGO THE BOLDEST IMAGINATION COULD NOT HAVE DREAMT."
> Henry George

On the subject of tropical cities, which is where I can make my best contribution, in particular for the areas that are still empty, where it is possible to create utopian cities that then become "topian" because then they have a space. It permits us to re-enchant the world, to reinvent it from the tropics. It's a possibility to make a harmonic city with a size of 20,000 to 30,000 inhabitants. This is a scale that still permits nature to recover from the contamination and pollution that those kind of cities produce. At the same time, it permits us to not surpass the biological speed that is bicycles and pedestrians.

In addition, the ideal is to create a settlement that works at different levels with the local natural topography rather than changing it. The goal is to move the machines and vehicles of combustion engines underground, because the surface level should be for the human beings and the other animal nature kingdoms.

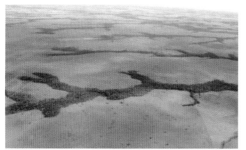

Of course, one has to draw on "geometric imagination" because the crisis of the city is fundamentally a crisis of imagination. That's the only dangerous desert, the desert of imagination.

In order to invoke the will of the settlers of these last frontiers, we have proposed not to call them urban settlements, because I don't believe in urbanism. I believe more in "ruralism" that is not strictly dispersed ruralism, but is also not as concentrated as the urbanism that we know. Obviously, without surpassing that scale I mentioned earlier, 30,000 inhabitants.

Our ecological footprint at Gaviotas is designed for the savannahs of the Orinoco Basin and the plains of South America, located between the Tropic of Cancer and Capricorn. We gave them very suggestive names. One has to enchant human beings so they can create new utopias where people from all countries of the world can be participants, not just spectators. I believe to the extent that people mix and races mix, we can achieve a sustainable peace, because war, for me, is the failure of intelligence. Right now, it looks like we are in a sustainable failure.

The Regreening of the Americas

Lugari: At the same time, these cities should be the catalysts, the poles, of the re-greening of the planet, so that we combat the baldness of the earth, so that the biomass easily reaches 50% of the nonsubmerged earth. Much more important than facing the simple global warming, originated by the increased carbon dioxide of cultural origin, is to protect the structure, the chemical composition of the whole atmosphere, which is a combination of 70% of nitrogen, 21% of oxygen, and a few other chemical elements. The issue of global warming, although it is important, nonetheless is a reductionist and fragmented form of reasoning. A much more transcendent issue is that this structure of the atmosphere be maintained. It is directly linked to the quantity of biomass and the structure of living beings on the planet. First, there was life, and then atmosphere. If life, which is the biomass, which is 99% of vegetable plant origin, goes below 30%, the seriousness lies not within the fact that the earth is warming, but whether life for humans fundamentally, will still be possible.

There is a magnificent book by Alan Weisman about this, **The World Without Us**, that describes how life would be on the planet without the most irritable species, which is us. These new cities therefore must be the focal points that convene the people for this important battle against the baldness of the earth. That's the only war that I can justify. The struggle should be something of the same transcendence, the same importance, as the one that happened when President John F. Kennedy called on the will of the American people. In this case, it would be a message to the whole world, to travel to the moon.

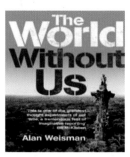

Going back, we have suggested names like the **City of the New Millennium, the Re-Enchanted City, the Reborn City, Felicitas, the Sensible City, the Illuminated City, BioCity and Music, Vitalitas, Tropicalus**. Obviously, these settlements, more than cities, have to be of mixed use. The big mistake of Le Corbusier, one of the most important architects of history, was when he compartmentalized and sectioned off the city. He said, "In this part of the city, one studies; in this part of the city, one works; and this part of the city, one does commerce; and this part of the city is the government and the institutions."

Instead of having an organic mixture that would have avoided 90% of the transportation costs that has to be used to overcome this breaking up of the city. The cities of the future should be surrounded by a food production ring. It is absurd that those of us in the community eat products that come from thousands and thousands of kilometers away. In organic cities, it's not necessary to surpass biological speed, but in the case that it does happen, it should be a public and collective transport system. There is no sense in inventing the car, as it was done in Germany, because now the car is reinventing the human being. It doesn't make sense. It's time to free ourselves from the internal

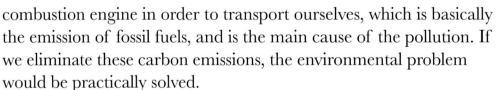

combustion engine in order to transport ourselves, which is basically the emission of fossil fuels, and is the main cause of the pollution. If we eliminate these carbon emissions, the environmental problem would be practically solved.

For me, this is nothing utopian. If 100 years ago, we had met and we had to design the world such as it is today, everyone would've said that we were utopian. Now here we are and I don't know if it's for better or for worse. The installed capacity of the world, which is the most important one, should solve the most fundamental problems, not a cosmetic technology.

Therefore, one has to understand that the roof of a family potentially and scientifically can generate all the energy that this family consumes.

I don't know how human intelligence, despite bureaucracy, was able to go to the moon and could send sensors to space to different planets of the solar system-but has not been able to give sufficient priority to creating nonpolluting cities with renewable energy. We have to go back to the elemental, to the substantial. Our education is sophisticated in things technological, but without any transcendent goals. This is the message that we want to give out of Gaviotas. In the immensity of the Colombian plains, in a place that's far from everything and close to nothing, it's an extraordinary place where one can think like in the time of Socrates.

Zelov: I read in the Alan Weisman book about Gaviotas that the idea of human happiness is a vital part of the equation for your development. Can you talk a little bit about that?

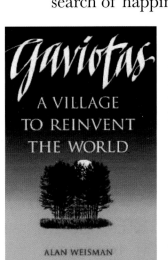

Lugari: We at Gaviotas, we bet on technology as an instrument for the search of happiness, as Thomas Jefferson said. There is no sense in development for development's sake. At one time, in Popayan, in my native city in Colombia, a big French thinker arrived. My father invited him to have a mental exercise in my home and it was being translated because he didn't speak Spanish. The important thing of dialogue is not what one side thinks or what the other side thinks, but the emergence, the new concepts that result from this dialogue. In very simple words, we arrived to this temporary conclusion: If you need roads, have them. If you want all the cybernetics, have them. If you need all kinds of development and infrastructure, have it. If this only generates progress and not happiness, then why do you have them? The big challenge of the city of the future is a symbiosis of progress and happiness.

> " NOTHING IS UNTHINKABLE, NOTHING IMPOSSIBLE TO THE BALANCED PERSON, PROVIDED IT COMES OUT OF THE NEEDS OF LIFE AND IS DEDICATED TO LIFE'S FURTHER DEVELOPMENT."
> Lewis Mumford

Zelov: I also read in the Gaviotas book that music is a big part of your community. Can you explain why?

Lugari: I believe that music is something fundamental as a background. It's one of the basic elements for sustainability, to the search for happiness, and a guarantee for peace. The human being always will have instincts. The human being is a mixture of reason and nonreason. Music is the harmonious bridge between these two components of the human being. Cities should be designed from music.

> " MUSIC IS THE HARMONIOUS VOICE OF CREATION; AN ECHO OF THE INVISIBLE WORLD."
> Giuseppe Mazzini

Zelov: Do you encourage everybody to play music at Gaviotas?

Lugari: Yes. In Gaviotas, almost everybody plays. Of course, it's a completely free community. Musical instruments are played, and we seek harmony in multiple dimensions. Often, when we go to harvest in the forest, we do it as we sing or interpreting pieces of the tropical plains, because sustainability is linked to the state of the soul. Music and gesture was the first language of humankind.

Zelov: It's connected to the creative process at Gaviotas, music and the creative process?

Lugari: In Gaviotas, music is something permanent and daily, and it's built into the daily life so that people do it naturally and don't notice it, like the creativity.

Zelov: You have a particular philosophy of creativity. It seems to be very much in line with experimental design approach.

Lugari: Creativity in Gaviotas is taught within an informal environment. There is no committee of creativity. I have never called a formal meeting to discuss it. I've never written a memorandum on the subject. The environment of the community is such that creativity is the result of an organic process, not an ordered one. It's a little bit like the original creativity within chaos, which later on permits us to form a cosmos. When the cosmos is not appropriated for specific circumstances, we turn to the chaos so that then we may build with a puzzle and a different cosmos. We believe in the famous saying of Heraclitus, who said that the only permanent thing is change. This enables us to say that maturity exists in realizing one's dreams. If someone doesn't dream, it's because they're asleep. In Gaviotas, we're always dreaming and realizing.

That's part of what Gaviotas can teach a city in the 21st century in terms of creativity, in terms of eco-development, teaching the 21st century city in Gaviotas. More than teaching, because we don't believe that things are exactly replicable, we can inspire, transmit and convey a form of thinking that believes the cities should be systemic within a scale that is harmonious with its environment, and that it live from the interests of nature without affecting nature.

Zelov: You seem to find inspiration from the ancient Greek city. Is there a specific city? What about ancient Greece?

Lugari: I refer to the Socratic and pre-Socratic epochs of Greece, because curiously, all these ideas emerged

in small settlements and small cities. Gaviotas, to a certain extent, is like a little city-state. It is neither very well communicated nor totally un-communicated. In North America, where there are obligatory texts, it is called a city. However, it's neither totally connected nor totally isolated, and since it doesn't have obligatory, mandatory texts, we can think with tropical criteria, and have arrived at the rediscovery of the tropics on it's own terms. Since there are no formalities, we believe that creativity is the biggest gift of the human being. We can get out of the box, be informal, and the informality produces very intense dialogues that are given every day in frequent interchanges in the dining rooms of Gaviotas, where the entire community is creating without prima donnas.

Zelov: Can you talk about some of your innovations at Gaviotas?

Lugari: In Gaviotas, we work in many disciplines. In Gaviotas, we are giving rebirth to tropicality. One of the most revealing examples of this proposition, just to speak about one of many, is the establishment of a tropical bio-diverse forest. Twenty-five years ago, we planted 8000 hectares of tropical forest, which is now the largest planted forest in Colombia. It is also in a place where everybody said it was not possible to do, according to the established academic criteria at the time. When we did, we established a tropical pine, not a northern pine, but a Caribbean pine forest, the seeds of which we collected in the forests of the ancient Mayan civilization of Guatemala, Nicaragua, and Honduras. It is associated with a fungus at the roots of the tree, mycorrhiza, which created a symbiosis which enabled this forest to be a thriving forest full of vitality. At the same time,

> "THE CREATIVE PERSON IS BOTH MORE PRIMITIVE AND MORE CULTIVATED, MORE DESTRUCTIVE, A LOT MADDER AND A LOT SANER, THAN THE AVERAGE PERSON."
> Frank Barron

it created the environmental conditions for certain local native species that were dormant during thousands of years to be reborn, to re-merge, and create a forest of 200 different species, in which the tropical pine of the Mayan was simply the initial leader.

Zelov: I read that you invented a wind turbine. You're turning wind into electricity.

Lugari: Not for electricity, for water pumping. Let's talk about this. One of the fundamental issues of any settlement is water. Civilization has been a permanent dialogue of mankind with water. The first thing that we did when we started out in Gaviotas was to buy a motor pump to extract water. Obviously, it had a lot of problems. It wasn't adequate. It wasn't appropriate for that location. We then fertilized. In Gaviotas, we don't order. We fertilized the imagination to develop a windmill to extract water that, in Gaviotas' case, is at 50 meter of depth. Therefore, Gaviotas is not a desert, but that location was a desert of imagination. We developed a technology that was a very high technology, but appropriate. For me, sometimes technology is sophisticated in the research, but if the result, the outcome, is not simple, it's not high technology. One of the

characteristics of this windmill, besides its light weight of 70 kilos, is that it doesn't need a vein to orient itself in the wind. It self-orients itself because of the geometrical design of the wings, or the oars. It's a double action effect because it pumps water when the piston goes up, as well as when the piston goes down. Another project is the one of solar water heaters. We developed the solar water

heater in Gaviotas, despite the fact that it's a warm, tropical climate, because Bogota is also in the tropics, but it's a cold, tropical climate. We developed the first solar heater for a health clinic in Gaviotas, because the warm water was fundamental. Then, after a few years, we extended this type of solar heating to the rest of Colombia, to the extent that we have today about 40,000 solar heaters installed approximately, which corresponds to a power plant of about 65,000 kilowatts. This technology of the solar heater works with a siphonal thermal technology. It's in other words like a natural computer and it has no moving parts, and it's maintenance is practically nil. These solar heaters from Gaviotas produced economic profits because it is a systemic product with the funds all joined together. Gaviotas is a foundation. It works like an ecosystem where the cooperation replaces hierarchy. Since Gaviotas is a systemic project with united funds, single budget, the economic profits generated by the value added to Gaviotas is what enabled us to begin to plant the forest. Fundamentally, in this sense, all of Gaviotas is a solar energy. A forest is one of the most genuine ways of capturing solar energy and to capture carbon, of course. All electricity in Gaviotas is generated through culling of the forest, not the cutting but the culling. We have small hydraulic systems of power generation. The heat is created with solar panels, solar water panels, and the vapors go to the factory for gum rosin; and it all comes from the culling of the forest. There are many mechanisms that use just muscle power, manual pumps of all kinds. All of Gaviotas has a design in its architecture and of its ruralism that's bioclimatic. We design and build our installations using a bioclimatic intelligence that has worked very well, instead of simply plugging in to our fossil source. I am very astounded here in Philadelphia, despite the fact that we are in the springtime, which is at an ideal temperature with a perfect air conditioning naturally, that we're still using air conditioning during this season because we have a cultural activism that doesn't correspond to any logic. I call this cultural contamination.

> "THE PRINCIPLE GOAL OF EDUCATION IS TO CREATE MEN WHO ARE CAPABLE OF DOING NEW THINGS, NOT SIMPLY OF REPEATING WHAT OTHER GENERATIONS HAVE DONE - MEN WHO ARE CREATIVE, INVENTIVE AND DISCOVERERS."
> Jean Piaget

Zelov: The prison of modernism.

Lugari: Yes, it makes no sense. This cannot be called engineering, because engineering comes from genius, in a word, ingenious. Also, a grave error is made. The universities keep on issuing certificates without an expiration date in a world where technology is permanently changing. It stays in the text because it doesn't have cultural acceptance. This is a crisis of useful energy, because there is no lack of energy. A crisis is not an absence of resources, but the nonutilization of imagination accompanied with enthusiasm. It's a crisis that we have deliberately created, because we know there are alternatives and solutions, many of them presented by Amory Lovins. In a deliberate and conscientious way, we have a very unintelligent scheme that is anti-economic, despite the fact that there are alternatives. It's not an energy crisis. There is no energy crisis, because energy is not created nor destroyed, but it's a human crisis, a brain crisis.

> " HUMAN SUBTLETY WILL NEVER DEVISE AN INVENTION MORE BEAUTIFUL, MORE SIMPLE OR MORE DIRECT THAN DOES NATURE BECAUSE IN HER INVENTIONS NOTHING IS LACKING, AND NOTHING IS SUPERFLUOUS."
> Leonardo da Vinci

Zelov: Part of Gaviotas' philosophy is to develop the creativity of every person to engage in the inventive process?

Lugari: Yes, one time, we had some foreign visitors who came to Gaviotas. They were of French origin. People like things to be defined for them. For me, there's nothing more absurd than a dictionary, because a dictionary is static; but nonetheless, for their mental convenience, they insisted that I define Gaviotas. I said what I said at the beginning of my talk, Gaviotas is the permanent quest for temporary truths. They didn't like the definition. Then we talked a little. We got into the administrative structure of Gaviotas, which works like an ecosystem where there is cooperation and not competition. I told them that in Gaviotas, there are 200 people working, but there are also 200 people thinking, whereas in traditional, institutional, industrial society, there are only 10 people thinking and hundreds of people just working. The future of humanity has to involve the collective wisdom of every person.

> " THE ROLE OF THE TEACHER IS TO CREATE THE CONDITIONS FOR INVENTION RATHER THAN PROVIDE READY-MADE KNOWLEDGE."
> Seymour Papert

Zelov: Can principles of Gaviotas can they be translated into the modern American city, for instance Philadelphia?

Lugari: I don't speak of principles. I don't talk of axioms, but that the world is ever changing. The mental approach with which Gaviotas analyzes problems, its analytical architecture, can serve as its inspiration, not as a norm to help for cities to become self-sustaining. We are not a school. We can't replicate Gaviotas. We can aspire but not replicate.

Zelov: In 100 years, how would you like people to think about Gaviotas?

Lugari: First, every time that I give a talk, if they don't tell me at the end of the talk that I have illusions, I feel like I wasted my time. Big developments can't have been made without dreams, without hopes. Never has a pessimist changed the world. When a pessimist is asked to choose between two evils, he keeps both of them. I am seeing a scenario that has made a pact with hope. I am not a wizard and I do not know what will be happening with Gaviotas in 100 years, but it's very possible that there might be left a record or a way of living that will have shown to humanity, and the tropics in particular, how to evolve without destroying while always pursuing happiness.

Zelov: That's part of the reason for the name Gaviotas, a seabird?

Lugari: Yes. Gaviotas is a name that came up by chance. It's not a traditional name. It's not a linear name. A more linear name would've been a center for research and development within the tropics, but the first nonlinearity of Gaviotas was its name. Also, because in Gaviotas there are many river gulls. It's a symbol of freedom, because in Gaviotas, we believe that without freedom, we will never fight poverty, because imagination without liberty has no place. These days, I've been giving some talks in Bogota. If we look at the planet like an enterprise, a total enterprise, like the astronauts saw it, we say that higher education and business administration is failing, because it's not possible that an enterprise is capable of sustainably producing 60% of poverty permanently and compromising its national capital. That is putting its own life in danger long term. At the same time, this is more to be criticized in the tropical corridor, because there you have the highest index of biological productivity; but ironically, it accompanies the highest index of poverty in the world, which didn't happen thousands of years ago. I say that's the miracle of poverty, because where it's impossible to be poor, that's where we are poor. It's the miracle of poverty, and all of it is a mental attitude. As I said, 200 years ago, Latin America was much more advanced than North America in all fields. Now it's the exact opposite. Of course, these are important problems of pollution, but I believe that humanity will enter into a pact of imagination to re-green the planet.

" O! FOR A MUSE OF FIRE, THAT WOULD ASCEND THE BRIGHTEST HEAVEN OF INVENTION."
William Shakespeare

CHAPTER 10

The St. Andrews

Conversation

with

Graham Leicester

+ Tony Hodgson

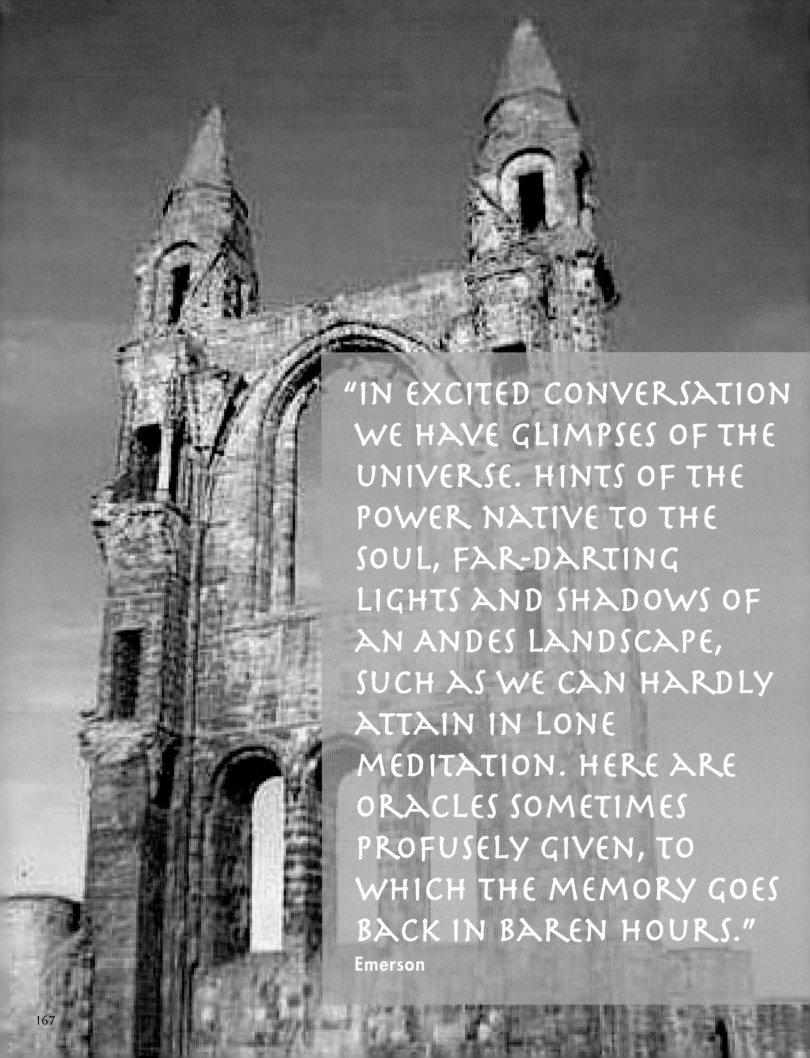

"IN EXCITED CONVERSATION WE HAVE GLIMPSES OF THE UNIVERSE. HINTS OF THE POWER NATIVE TO THE SOUL, FAR-DARTING LIGHTS AND SHADOWS OF AN ANDES LANDSCAPE, SUCH AS WE CAN HARDLY ATTAIN IN LONE MEDITATION. HERE ARE ORACLES SOMETIMES PROFUSELY GIVEN, TO WHICH THE MEMORY GOES BACK IN BAREN HOURS."

Emerson

167

Learning how to think about the future in a broad minded manner is crucial to participating in creating the Future City. The chapter consists of a conversation with Grahm Leicester and Tony Hodgson of the International Futures Forum. Read carefully and observe how they gently weaves in and illuminate some of the key aspects of the futurist thought process.

<u>Some of the themes explored herewithin include:</u>

-Learning Journey's

-Thinking Sandwich

-3rd Horizon Thinking

-The Search for the 2nd Enlightenment

 -The Scale of the Present Moment of any Being is in the relation to the extent of their conciousness

-The Implicate Order

-The Power of Visualization

-Policy is Learning

-Designing the Future

This is a conversation is the ancient (14c) sense of the word to "turn about with." May you the reader's world be expanded and transformed by the content within this conversation.

CZ

Chapter 10:
The St. Andrews Conversation

Phil Cousineau: The painter Piet Mondrian, who once described one of the inspirations to create art as "the nostalgia for the future." What do you think is inside creative people that compels them to yearn for something that doesn't yet exist?

Graham Leicester: Those of us at the The International Futures Forum have been working for some time to answer the central question of how do we take more effective action in a world that's become so complex that we no longer understand it and we can't control it. How do we act effectively? To help us answer these questions we developed a set of "nudge cards." These cards are prompts for shifting us out of the normal ways of thinking that are based on control and understanding, the perfect understanding. In a complex circumstance that you find difficult to make sense of, what are some of the prompts for how to think about it, how to make sense of it, what kinds of attitudes and behaviors to show in those circumstances? The card I turned over now says, "Develop a future consciousness to inform the present."

> Work with the creative impulse in any situation

> Develop a future consciousness to inform the present

We talked a lot in the International Futures Forum about why do we need this. Why do we need to get to grips with the present? Answer, because there are some big, challenging, looming issues that actually threaten the future. There's a lot of futures literature, which is pretty much about dystopia. It's no longer utopia and it's no longer inspirational, it's threatening. There's a lot of conversation about sustainability. We asked ourselves in the IFF, "sustainability of what, for what purpose?" Mere survival actually doesn't inspire any of us. It would be a start, but it's not enough. Our sense of future consciousness is that the thing that we want to and need to maintain and sustain is human aspiration. I think that's the nostalgia for the future. The nostalgia for me too is about looking for the inspiration in the

> " CONSCIOUSNESS IS THE TEMPLE IN MAN."
> R.A. Schwaller de Lubicz

past, which is a source of inspiration and imagination. There are very few things that we can dream about that have not been dreamt about in the past. With a lot of the so-called futuristic schemes, you'll find many precursors. One of my favorite quotes is "If you want a new idea, read an old book."

Tony Hodgson: I can build on that. What is this nostalgia? That is a word, which is often associated with a kind of harking back to the good old days. If you translate it more as yearning, what is it that we yearn for that is related to our observation that things are not what we'd like them to be? What that tends to lead to and what in the IFF we call the first enlightenment consciousness, which says, "Let's get it organized. Let's get it under control. Let's do something about it." Those who are saying that are a minority speaking on behalf, or believing they speak on behalf of the majority. Looking at it from a different perspective, looking at this little card, it says on it facilitate self-organization. Now, if we treat every human being as a self that has inherent in them, somewhere this yearning, then what perhaps would be more effective is to appeal to that yearning for a better future in a way that is surrounded by enabling conditions. That is, conditions which enable people to organize themselves. It's very interesting, you've spent some time recently visiting the new Scottish Parliament, that was an attempt to get some degree of

> "LOCK-AND-KEY. THE DISTINGUISHING DEVICE OF CIVILIZATION AND ENLIGHTENMENT."
> Ambrose Bierce

Facilitate self-organisation

devolution so Scotland could become a more self-organizing community in relation to education possibly, and healthcare to some degree, and certain other aspects like transportation and so on. This little symbol here is a flower. What a beautiful self-organizing entity a flower is. Symbolically, I can remind myself of future consciousness that facilitates self-organization.

Leicester: It's worth saying something here about Scotland, and this goes back into another of the organizing principles for our thinking about complexity and messy confusion. We've been looking at the kinds of devices that we do use to get to grips with that kind of system, system science, complexity science, chaos theory, there's all of that, but there's also the artistic intuitive set of capacities as well. Narrative storytelling, metaphor and myth, which you'll be very familiar with, as ways of making sense of complex reality. We looked back to the myth and the metaphor of the enlightenment, because we're based in Scotland. We wanted an international effort that would attract people to Scotland for a conversation about making sense of the modern world. The enlightenment metaphor was the perfect introduction for that. We came up with this idea, actually a new myth, **the myth of the second enlightenment**. We concluded that what we need right now is what happened 250 years or so ago, which was rapid technological advance, growth of trade and travel, growing interconnectedness, and an accelerated speed of change. With the birth of the Industrial Era, a whole group of people were saying we no longer understand how the world works. Then a group of philosophers, merchantmen, scientists, all got together over a period of about 30 years in many different countries around Europe, some of them in Scotland, and came up with a set of rules for how that kind of society worked. We've pretty much been living off those thinkers ever since. Part of our new myth says that we're in exactly the same position. We too are subject to rapid technological change, new interconnectedness, speed of advance; we are in a world we don't understand anymore. The old rules no longer seem to apply. The new rules haven't been discovered. **What we need is a second enlightenment**. We think we need to force feed this.

We can't just wait for it to emerge as it did last time. We will force feed it perhaps in the same way that others did back in the 18th century. We invited a group of people to Scotland to participate in this conversation, and we drew the parallel with the first enlightenment, and said this was a creative, collaborative, interdisciplinary conversation that went on for many years, and so will ours be. We'll set ourselves a couple of years to start with. We have no end in sight. We want to get to a better understanding of how the world works. Full stop. The test of whether that is a better understanding of how the world works will be effectiveness in action. If we can take action in the face of some of these pressing contemporary challenges, the kinds of actions that have eluded us up to now, then we'll know that we're getting a better sense of how the world really is today. That was the myth that brought people to Scotland and has kept people in this conversation. Tony, I don't know if you want to continue the story from there.

Hodgson: One consequence of taking enlightenment a bit seriously is that you can't dissociate it from learning. I think one of the interesting things in our experience over this five years is the rate of learning that we as a network of people have been experiencing. This is very interesting because most all the members are rather influential people in their fields, who are normally in the role of being the expert with the answer. Yet in this IFF culture that we've developed, we're all kids trying to discover new territory. We are pretty humbled by it, which enables us to have quite different kinds of conversations than you get in academia or business, where many of us hang out. This has really led to a kind of thinking sandwich that we've developed around learning. A typical plenary get together, I like to use the Scottish term gathering, as in the gathering of the clans, we have a gathering once a year, as well as other little projectss, in which we we start with learning journeys. If we want to be grounded in experience, let's go have some. Let's go and visit some people and places, which are out of the usual realm of our encounters. We've had some very creative and helpful people set us up with journeys that expose us to quite new stuff that we have to take in. Then we go away into a digestive phase and we mull over and share our reflections on our experience. We relate that at one level to our sort of conceptual models, at another level to how we're feeling about things, and at another level of how this might impact on our own experience of doing things. That usually leads to some kind of gathering of ideas and information, which we facilitate quite strongly using visual techniques. The problem with really good conversations is that they can easily disappear out the air conditioning and evade capture. Capturing the essence of conversations has become very important for us. Indeed the playing cards we invented contain a nugget of conversation from some meeting or other that struck people as, oh, that's got something to it. The third part of the sandwich is, I guess the simple way to describe it is projects. There are people in our network both in Scotland and elsewhere, so in January this year we were in India for an encounter like this, whcrc thcrc's a mutual recognition that they have a messy, intractable, unsolvable challenge, a situation that hasn't yielded to the usual first enlightenment means. We say we'll come and learn about it with you. We don't have any solutions. We're not consultants. We won't sort of analyze it and give you the answer, but if you invite us in, you'll probably experience relating with your own situation differently. This has gradually caught on and so there are a number of areas where we've put out our emerging second enlightenment tentacles and touched the world to see if something different will begin to happen.

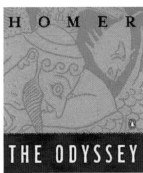

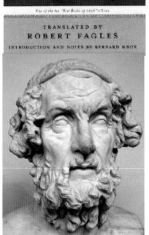

HOMER

THE ODYSSEY

TRANSLATED BY
ROBERT FAGLES

Cousineau: This reminds me of one of the great metaphors in western culture, the Odyssey. What your describing is more than a journey; it's an Odyssey. In my understanding, the origins of the word nostalgia goes all the way back to Homer. Historians tell us he was inspired by the nostois, the "returning home stories," which were told by thousands and thousands of sailors who made it home after great ordeals at sea. There's something profoudly deep in that word nostalgia that is more than sentimental. It's evokes a deep yearning to go home again--because that is where the answers are. I'm hearing an echo of this in your descriptions of the second enlightenment.

Leicester: It sparks a few thoughts for me. One is about the life cycle which is always journeying home, which I think we've forgotten. Most wisdom traditions have an idea of the stages of man. I think we were in India where the Hindu philosophy says there's a stage in your life when you've taken care of your family, when you start to take care of society. The rest of us look at Indian business practice and say look at them doing all of this stuff that we would call corporate social responsibility. Actually, they're just doing that because they're Hindu and that's the stage of life that they've reached. We shouldn't be surprised, and yet we are because we're ignorant of that tradition.

The other thing I think is about the T.S. Eliot quote about going back to the same place, but knowing it for the first time. We may all be going home, but it's going to be a very different home from the one that we imagined we were going to. I'm not one of those who's looking for the future in the past. I'm sure the future will look very different from the past, but we will recognize some of those deep components. We will recognize it as home. I'm also dubious about this notion of the future, if the truth be told. When we started this operation, we called it the International Futures Forum because it was about thinking of the challenges that face us in the present, but if we don't sort them out, we're going to have quite a miserable future.

Yet, some of the juice has gone out of that word future, even in the last five or six years I would say. The future is now an excuse, it's a place where you go to avoid action, or it's a place that is not worth going because we don't have time to go there. This kind of delivery, delivery, delivery, action orientation of today's culture doesn't allow us to think about the future, and I spend a lot of my time now saying we are not a futures organization. What we're doing is trying to understand the present better so that we can take action today that will contribute to a better future.

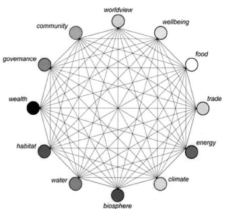

Hodgson: This question about the status of the future is very interesting. One of my mentors had this very interesting idea that time was complex (not simply one linear chronology) beyond even the Einsteinian sense of the space-time continuum where time itself was multidimensional. This was well before the physicists started playing around with string theory and dimensional space. In this view of the world, there are greater or lesser present moments and the scale of the present moment of any being is the extent of their

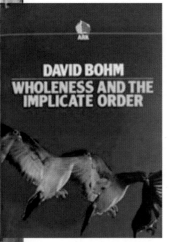

consciousness. A person with a large present moment is simultaneously conscious of the span of the past and the span of the future in the present, and therefore is able to act quite differently, because such a consciousness can see the consequences of their actions or inactions. I like the idea that if we want a better future, we have to discover it in the present. Things like learning journeys, which are in a sense a kind of modern form of pilgrimage in a way, are ways of expanding our consciousness so we can be more alert to the future that's already here. Now, if the future's already here, why are things such a mess if there's a good future around? When you begin to take a more flexible view of time in which the pattern of the future may be here, but there's something called realization, which is how is it brought into being. The Physicist David Bohm's idea was that in the present may be contained the whole of the future. It isn't so much a matter of predicting the future as unearthing or unfolding the future. The richness of what Bohm called "the implicate order" suggests we've probably only explored the edges of time. Perhaps one way of looking at creative acts of design and development is where somebody has stumbled across or been inspired by another bit of the hidden order that can then come into being and manifest. This is a completely different way of looking at the future from the prediction or even the scenario thinking point of view. I can't say that in IFF, we've only sort of touched the hand of this thing, but it does seem to me that part of the struggle we have is that we need to place the word future in the context of a second enlightenment consciousness. We get really stuck if we keep using it in the context of the first enlightenment consciousness. Part of what we try and do in our conversations is to gently remind each other when we're slipping back into the old ways, the old paradigm, which we're all very good at doing because that's where we got our training.

Another aspect of the future then I think that I'd like to bring is this idea that we don't understand the structure of the present. We certainly don't understand the structure of the present as something which is holistic, something which is a whole. One field that we've been very interested in, and some of us over a lifetime, is system science and systems thinking. What we've tried to do in some of our work is to look for ways of representing what we're investigating as connected wholes. Indeed, David Lorimer, one of our members, has drawn our attention to a whole field that's emerging that we could summarize as the ethics of interconnectedness.

Visualizing The Future

Cousineau: Because we're in Scotland I'm finding a parallel between futurists and golfers, which is the ability to visualize the future. In Michael Murphy's famous book, Golf in the Kingdom, his shamanistic golf pro, Shivas Irons, tells his young student that unless you learn how to visualize, you will fall into old habits. Only by visualizing, Shivas says, will you be live up to your potential. It will require years of practice in which you have to picture yourself creating the perfect golf swing. Otherwise, there is a retreat and we know this all the way back to the Greeks, unless we push ourselves, we fall into old habits. Think about that in terms of the implication for futurists and designers and architects. Unless we teach ourselves how to visualize the future, we will continue to fall into old habits and make the same mistakes over and over again. What role does visualization play in your futurist thinking?

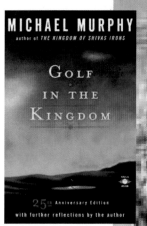

Leicester: One of the things we spoke about first in setting up the International Futures Forum was ways of looking at where are the challenges to our understanding of the present world. We came up with the concept of "Four Pillars" to describe where we've lost our sense of understanding how the world works. The first pillar was government, and this was around 2000, so the sort of signature question was who really won the U.S. election and does it even matter? The fact that you can ask that kind of question shows the crisis in governments. The second pillar was sustainability. How come there are so many things that we know are unsustainable and yet we keep on doing them, and can't seem to ever stop or to innovate other ways of doing them. The third pillar was the economy. In spite of all the bookshelves groaning with tomes about the new rules for the new economy, we still don't understand how the new economy works. Adam Smith certainly wouldn't understand it. The fourth pillar was consciousness. This pointing to really basic questions like "What does it mean to be a human being?" In the past might have been only academic, philosophical issues, but are now more palpable. For example, do clones get the vote? Consciousness was always one of the areas that we needed to dig more deeply into. At IFF we've been doing some practical work on mental illness, that was brought to our attention by the World Economic Forum. I prefer to call it a growing epidemic of mental distress.

You can see the figures for this in breakdown or burn out in families, in communities, in societies. The Harvard psychologist, Robert Kegan, wrote a great book about this back in the early '90s called In Over Our Heads: The Mental Demands of Modern Life. Essentially, it was about our level of consciousness as a society and what we are able to cope with, or what we've been trained to cope with. For the last couple of hundred years, we have been able to get by on a level four consciousness, and now the world is throwing us so much stuff that we need a level five. The IFF has said from the start that some kind of evolution in consciousness is necessary in order to cope with the complexities of the present. That's how I would describe the story of the Golf in the Kingdom, which is actually about increasing your level of consciousness, your awareness of who you are, where you are, who you are being in the present. Brian Goodwin, another of our members from Schumacher College, said right from the start of our futures inquiry, that the art of creating the future is learning how to live more deeply in the present. That's the evolution of consciousness. That's the psychological level of being able to cope with the world that we don't understand and can't control. I could go onto a whole other riff about how that shows up in organizations, and we might get onto that later, because I think that's one of the things that makes it difficult for our traditional organizations to take on new ideas and to embrace what Buckminster Fuller called "design outlaws." Tony, do you want to say something about the visualization element?

Hodgson: Yes. I think that's very important. The interesting thing about visualization is it's operating whether we are aware of it or not. The conclusion we came to, which was highlighted very much, given that our second meeting of the IFF was immediately after 9/11, was the role of fear in driving people's imagination and the power of imagination to bring about what it is imagined. Therefore, the vicious cycle of fear, bad things, more fear, bad things, which also relates to the question of control because it's been well known by tyrants for many centuries that fear is a good way to control people. We see ourselves entering into a world of more and more fear-making under "the guise of war on terror," and other such inventions to keep this control, in a world that we don't understand and can't control. For us, we see it almost like the last thrashing of the tail of the old order, which likes to call itself a new order, using the old methods to control. Whereas we see that the other side of the imagination, the active side, is grounded in love. At IFF, we talked about being caught in the "fear loop," where we can succumb to the stressful things in life. We talked about the love loop, which is the way to sustain human aspiration in a world that we don't understand and can't control because love doesn't need to control. Love needs to love. From that aspect of the imagination, we can then nurture our imagination with desire, and if our desire is based on, let's call it good ethics to keep it simple, then this desirable world becomes the loving attention that we give to what we do now that will bring about a better future.

What increasingly we find ourselves working on is trying to visualize the kinds of futures which will match the conditions that we see that we're entering into. Whether it's the sustainability level of how do seven or eight billion people live with the footprint which is respectful to Gaia. How do we develop government systems that are able to treat policy as a learning process? Policy today seems to have the fashion of being where it's rational, which it often isn't, but where it is rational, it's the rationality of evidence-based policy. Which is rather like saying we're going down an unknown road with unknown geography and we're going to drive in the rear view mirror. That is heading for a crash. Also, that policy needs to be informed not just by rules and guidelines. **Policy is learning.** How do we move governments into connection with the power of visualization for a better world? In the area known as Falkirk in Scotland here, we've made some overtures in this area that was going through quite a shakeup in its economic and social structure. At least for a short while I think, through interacting in this sort of learning way with some of the key people there, a more positive view emerged of the future and better things started happening. The other thing, which I think is very important in visualization, is what do we inform our visualization with? That's one of the things that attracted us to the idea of ecological design, that with the best of intentions, we can still be visualizing in the old paradigms that don't relate to our actual challenges and situation. We also have another activity that we're beginning to develop in IFF with the rather grand title of "World Modeling." This is really looking at the idea that came out of the Club of Rome initially, of the global problematique. You can't divide the world into packages of problems, solve those problems and expect to get a good result, because we don't understand the linkages and the feedback. We can only arrive at a resolutique, as they called it, in our view by this shift of consciousness and a new kind of visualization. Then I think you've got the

Goethian principle of providence comes to your aid if you're bold and dream and then you act. At a recent seminar in California, the opening remark of the workshop leader was a quotation from Jalal ad-Din Rumi, which is about doing a large and foolish project; it doesn't matter what people think. I think that's also something that we're now thinking about in IFF that having got this far, what's our next large and foolish project? When we heard about Ecological Cities, we thought that seems a very large and foolish project, we'd like to join with that.

Leicester: That's William Blake as well:

"If a fool would persist in his folly, he would become wise."

Sustainable Cities

Hodgson: The challenge of developing our cities so that they are ecologically sound, sustainable within the footprint of the planet seems to be perhaps on of the most complex, messy, wicked challenges that we have. I'd like to connect this back with visualization. What we've been experimenting with over the years in IFF and in other circles that we connect with, is increasing the ways that we can represent and picture these difficult, complex situations. There are two basic cognitive obstacles that we're up against, both of them discovered by Scottish psychologists. One by Miller is the famous seven, plus or minus two, that our brains seem to be constructed, that at least in short-term memory, we can only handle seven, plus or minus two ideas. However, the Lord in his wisdom didn't create the universe with only seven categories. We have vastly more complexity out there, how many variables would actually have to go through the mind of the mayor of the city of London, if he were able to handle it.

The second theory is by R.D. Laing, the psychiatrist, who made the point that we're not used to noticing the things that we don't notice, and because we don't notice what we don't notice, we're the victim of the consequences. Part of the difficulty of ecological design as we see it, is how do you expand the range of capability, not just of an individual, but a whole network of individuals, so that between them, the collaborative brain can be much more intelligent than the individual brains. This is very hard to do.

Another mentor of mine, who was head of group planning at Royal Dutch Shell, said that he was surprised how often he saw a group of highly intelligent individuals come together in a committee room and add up to one idiot. So we have a really interesting challenge here. We've found is that it's helpful to consider three different mindsets in relation to the future. The first mindset is we're looking at the future from the current belief system and paradigm, and we call that the "first horizon," which you can see if you picture the plains leading up to the mountains. Another mindset is where you've actually visualized a viable future, a sustainable future, which is based on quite different principles and rules, and you can see many of the experiments that you're investigating in your search for the ecological city are of that kind. We call those "third horizon mindsets." Now, to the first horizon mindset, third horizon is wacky, outlaw, off limits, impractical, etc. Now the interesting thing is that it isn't a simple transition from first horizon to third horizon, which is why they're numbered that way because in the middle is a second horizon. The second horizon is the very difficult transition zone where these two mindsets have to learn to talk to each other. For example, from the point of view of energy, we might say we'd like to have it all renewable and preferably by the end of the week so that we get rid of all the carbon emissions. How would society react if the lights don't stay on? So we have the predicament that how do we go through this transition zone. In fact, one of your American compatriots, Howard Kunstler, has written a book called **The Long Emergency** where he makes the case that what I've called "second horizon," would be something along the order of 30 years.

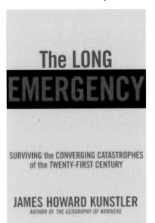

The Ecological City

Hodgson: Getting to the ecological city, even assuming we could move the infrastructure at that sort of pace, would be at least a generation, possibly two. How do we survive that transition? That is quite a journey. I don't think we'll ever be completely free of fossil fuels. We'll just be using it very wisely and modestly in the way that perhaps we should've thought of 100 years ago. Now, this is where "scenario thinking" can be helpful. One of the things that we've looked at is the idea of what's going to happen when the most advanced digital technology becomes increasingly embedded in the infrastructure. This may seem like a very first world kind of concern, excluding the third world, but on the other hand, it is interesting if you look at communities in Africa, which can be very traditional, and still have mobile phones. The idea that the technologies are alien to each other may be just a limitation that we're still under. Man, nature, technology may be able to relate in whole new ways that we haven't thought of yet. If you try and put intelligence into infrastructure, you're going to get two kinds of worlds. One is you're going to use it to fix today's problems, which is the driving in the rearview mirror. We call that scenario **Good Intentions**[1]. You will not miss the allusion to the road to hell is paved with those.

The other one is called **Faster, Faster**[2], which is that somehow we achieve the hydrogen economy, perhaps Iceland works and it sets a pattern for the rest of the world in different ways. We just carry on as we are getting faster and faster, whether we can handle the psychological stressors of that is another matter. However, supposing, as there is evidence, there is a rejection or a backlash about the technology. Then we find that the only

1. Good Intentions

possible way we can actually achieve the footprint that we want is to compress life into a completely new design of the city or urban environment. That becomes something we call **Urban Colonies Scenario**[3] which involves a change in community and culture.

The remaining one is **Tribal Trading**[4], where we get the full whack of peak oil, social breakdown and a full body version of Kunstler's long emergency. Very interestingly, in working through that one, which none of us wanted to look at, and in making ourselves work through it, we came up with some very positive elements. This could be a scenario, which itself is a transition, to even stronger communities, new forms of social

2. Faster, Faster

organization and completely different relationship of the concentrations of humanity in urban situations in general, what we in the western country would call the countryside or the landscape. None of those scenarios are predictions. The interesting thing is that you can look at any vision of the future you might have for any city. You could take the ones

3. Urban Colonies Scenerio

that have been investigated in your project and you can say supposing the world tends to go this way, what would that mean for achieving this kind of vision. On the other hand, if the world was to go this way, what would that mean? It becomes a very useful way of wind tunneling or testing out beforehand. What you're really trying to do is to imagine a future into the present and then check out what it's like there, and see what you can learn

4. Tribal Trading

from that. How can you improve your policies, your strategies, your technologies, your ways of social organization, to be more resilient? Resilience is the primary word, because we really in all honesty don't know what the future holds. All we know is that if we have a very narrow view of the future, we're definitely wrong. If we have a broad view of the future, we may get some bits of it right enough to be able to survive to figure out the bits we didn't understand. In a way, this scenario method provides a field for dialogue between the horizons.

Policy Making

Leicester: I've been thinking about three horizons in terms of policymaking inside government, because we take hope in a lot of innovators' talk about influencing the so-called policy process. We get the ideas in the manifestos, and get political parties to adopt them, get them embodied in legislation, have some kind of strategic policy statement that validates and legitimizes them. In my background, I used to work ingovernment. I was in the foreign service for 11 years, and I left government because I didn't see it working in that way. I thought maybe policymaking outside government might be more effective, and then I think as long as we stay in the same model of policymaking, then that's going to be no more effective than working inside the system. What I've come to understand since then about the policy process is that it does talked earlier about fear as a motivating force and I think that's overwhelmingly the case today in most developed world governments. I talked about the world of complexity and confusion, the world in which we are in over our heads. Psychologically, there are at least three dominant responses to being in over your head. One is the neurotic response when you deny the confusion, you say black is black, white is white, I do understand. I deny anything that I don't understand. This is the fight between good and evil, we'll go back to the old verities, the old certainties, we'll deny the confusion and we'll act with our model of simple reality. That's the neurotic response. There's a psychotic response as well that says, "Hell I don't understand what's going on anymore, I'm going to tune out and just eat, drink and be merry for tomorrow we die." I think that part of the futures discourse is playing into that psychotic response. Then there's the growth or the transformational response, which says, "Yes this is difficult; yes I don't understand; yes I'm confused, but I have certain human capacities, I've been in this kind of place before and it is possible to grow through this with enough help, support, patience, encouragement, love, care, attention, some of the things that are in short supply."

Now what I notice is that policymaking is almost exclusively in the neurotic response. The evidence of coming challenges is mounting and the response of policymakers and government generally, as an institution, is to become more and more neurotic, to deny that complexity and to deal with the simplicities. We are complicit. There's a lot of talk of blaming the media, but they are just selling to us and representing our views, which are also psychologically driven. We want simpler answers too. We can't cope with this confusion and so we demand simpler answers, and that's what we get, the kind of answers that are simple, arrogant and wrong.

That's one part of this. Actually, there's a wonderful book by Don Michael **On**

Learning to Plan and Planning to Learn written in the early 1970s. If I can paraphrase, the sole purpose of organization is to keep the turbulence outside at bay, to give us a zone of competence. The point of having organizations is to give us as individuals a zone of competence where we know what we do, we know how to do it,

we're confident of our success, we have peers around us and superiors who tell us that we're doing a good job, and however complex, confusing and messy the real world outside the organization gets, we have a zone There is third horizon thinking too, this kind of visionary, the visionary work that you do and that has it's place. Even some governments are developing that kind of work. The foresight project that Tony's talked about has developed some inspirational visions of the future. What's missing is the second horizon of policy work and the second horizon is where we innovate. We have now come to see that there are two forms of innovation. There's the kind of innovation that props up the existing system and allows it a few more years of life, a few more bumps of life. We see this in our current energy review in the U.K. for example, build a few more nuclear power stations that will plug the gap of the ones that we just lost. There's no innovational thinking there but there is a way that is innovative in that it is changing the present system in order to keep it, to encourage it's longevity. There's a second form of innovation, which is looking towards the visionary third horizon. It's actually starting to change the rules of the game. It's embedding in the present some new practice that is based on some different principles, that call about for a very different system and ecology in the future. I don't think we make that distinction in the policy world and I think it's very difficult to do that. An odd member of the IFF, Max Boisot, has written about this in terms of the entrepreneurial versus the managerial mindset, which I now see he actually has a description of versions of the second horizon. He talks maybe the third horizon would be the range of possible worlds, this is Jerome Bruner's work. **The third horizon is the domain of possible worlds.** In the second horizon, we have probable worlds that we can extrapolate the data from the present and suggest these things are likely to happen. We have probable worlds in which we can produce evidence. We can do evidence-based policy. We can make a case for making this innovation because we can point to some evidence from elsewhere and those are probable worlds. **Then we have plausible worlds.** The plausible worlds are the worlds that we can't see anywhere, we can't supply the evidence, but there's a plausible case that if we did these things, it might turn out this way. That's the world that we entrepreneur. That's the entrepreneurial mindset that can pitch the plausible world to the first horizon, to the powers that be and say look, let's try this. We have enough, it's plausible enough to give it a shot, but I can't prove it. In Max's work, he's looking at this difference between this entrepreneurial mindset that looks for plausibility and the managerial mindset that looks at probability. I'm afraid we can't get plausible worlds out of the probabilistic, managerial

mindset. That's been one of my learnings from the IFF time and time again. Indeed, why we do we keep reinventing so many of these wheels? Answer, because we pay so little attention to the policy process, so much attention to ideas and so little to the processes by which they're invented or by which they're generated, such as the psychological pressures on the individuals who are working inside the system. That's one of my reflections on this, the self-identification as outlaw. It's a kind of a psychological stance to put yourself outside of this dysfunctional system. Now, the in-laws, the people in the system, don't have that as an escape clause. They have to find their comfort in other ways. I'm afraid a perfect natural way of finding your comfort is to keep the system going and to keep making as good as possible a case for why it should keep going. The role of protecting the conventional wisdom is playing the same psychological function for the people inside the system as self-identification as outlaws is doing for the people who see themselves outside the system.

The Romance of the Design Outlaw

Cousineau: What about your fascination now with the outlaw becoming an in-law at some crucial point?

Leicester: I suppose I used to be an in-law and I've now become an outlaw, and we are always going home. Eventually, I will have to become an in-law again. Eventually, we have to make our accommodation with the system. No, hat's too didactic. I think there is a role for those who can make their accommodation with the system. Recently, there was a man in Scotland, who helped set up the big issue of a street newspaper. He started a conference prestentation I was at recently by saying I am a social entrepreneur. A social entrepreneur is the same as any other kind of entrepreneur. I break all the rules. I hate bureaucracy and I won't take no for an answer. Of course, he got a round of applause and much laughter. I think he's missing something. That is the role of the entrepreneur. The role of the social entrepreneur sooner or later has to engage with the rules, has to engage with the bureaucracy. Sure, yes, don't take no for an answer, but there is an accommodation that we have to make with the in-laws. The outlaws somehow have to meet the in-laws at some point, and I think that's going to be difficult. So long as wetake our psychological comfort from being outside the system, I think we limit our effectiveness in terms of shifting the process that operates inside.

Another thing that comes strongly out of the IFF work is once we began to understand our own process. We started to see what came out of it, and what comes out of our processes is insight, a fresh perspective, a fresh understanding into the way things are. Let's bottle that insight and sell it, and publish it and get it out there. We thought that an insight was an idea, but then we discovered that actually the insight lives in the people. The insight is a person. The insight is a subject and it's people who have those moments of insight who need support, not the ideas that need promulgating. The ideas can be promulgated too, but it's the people that need support. I think that's part of managing that outlaw/in-law interface in a more sophisticated way. I used to ramble on about what might be called a "traditional think tank," in which our role was to produce ideas and lob them over the wall into government. Predictably enough, when people see things coming over the wall, they duck. It just wasn't effective on either side, but now it's more person-to-person and it's looking for the people who are wanting to shift the metaphor because it's quite a nice one. In India, they talk about the fireflies and the buffaloes, rather than the outlaws and the in-laws. The fireflies are the spontaneous, local points of light-social entrepreneurs, and the buffaloes are the big bureaucracies.

What we see is that there are a lot of buffaloes out there who would like to take off their buffalo skins and reveal themselves as fireflies. I've come from this work from a background in policymaking inside government and I moved into what I call policymaking outside government. I've come to feel that neither is terribly effective, but a lot of my thinking has been about how to improve the lot of the people that are left behind. I met Tony soon after making my initial transition into policymaking outside government, so I've pretty much seen both sides of that landscape, and been on this journey of trying to make the connection back into what we might call the official policy process.

Hope for the Future

Cousineau: What have you learned from those observations that might give us some hope for the future?

" WITH REALIZATION OF ONE'S OWN POTENTIAL AND SELF-CONFIDENCE IN ONE'S ABILITY, ONE CAN BUILD A BETTER WORLD."
Dalai Lama

Hodgson: I think what I've learned is that we actually have to extend our capabilities even further and develop a capability to facilitate ecological design that embraces all of these horizons. Somehow, we have to be able to create conditions under which the in-laws and the outlaws can get together congenially and allow the creative juices to flow. Right now none of our institutions are capable of doing that. They're all pulling in different directions. They're all throwing things over the wall to each other and ducking. They don't have the collaborative capability to put the complexity together even around a simple vision. The two things that I would propose are, firstly, that we need a new kind of facilitator, what I call a third level facilitator. Level one is you can facilate people solving problems. Level two is you can facilitate people discovering what the problem is, and level three is you can actually help people shift paradigm. This is a sort of modern shamanic role in a way. In our a jargon at IFF, we call them social integrities. Social integrities, they're more powerful than networks, they're less ad hoc, but they're not institutionalized, they bring together the right minds in the right situations with the right alignment that can, as we used to say move mountains, but in this case, move cities. These days I'm becoming educated very rapidly because of my growing interest in this whole field of ecological design, sustainability, viability. We've inherited from these design

outlaws so many of the ingredients, even going back to Patrick Geddes and 100 years ago, brilliant examples of what we need. We have completely failed so far to work out the means whereby we bring the right people together in the right way in the right place to move it along in a way that actually has some slight chance of being commensurate with the unbelievable scale of the problem. An estimated 400 million people in China will be moving into megacities in the next 50 years. Never mind the ones we've already got that are going to have to adapt to climate change. I think this is an interesting basis for the encounter with your project because it seems like we're both needed, as well as a lot of other colleagues around the world who have equally necessary ingredients. This is not just a design problem, it's not just a social problem, it's not just an ecological problem, it's not just any kind of problem: it is the mother of all problems. This is basically trying to see how we could move the necessary design revolution that Buckminster Fuller made so clear in his latter years to have much more power behind it. We have to make it clear that we are not in the official sense of the term designers, but we're global citizens. This is becoming a passionate interest to us, because it does seem that it's hitting a nail on the head here.

Cousineau: Graham, from just a quick reflection, I am also wondering what you think we've learned in our adventure in IFF over the last five or so years. How you might sum up what might contribute to enabling a design revolution to take more energy and more possibilities?

Leicester: It's interesting that we lighted on the metaphor of the enlightenment and the idea of trying to search for a second enlightenment. It was only after we'd done that for about six months that we thought perhaps we ought to learn some lessons from how they did it the first time around. This is a huge agenda, and a huge challenge and a huge task. I wonder how the original enlightenment philosophers and others went about answering some of these pressing questions about how to understand the world. We found a wonderful guide in the figure of Alexander Brody, who occupies Adam Smith's chair of moral philosophy at Glasgow University and has written a wonderful book about the enlightenment. We invited him to dinner to talk to us about this. He identified in his book the three enabling conditions for the enlightenment. The first one was independent thinking, the willingness to challenge the conventional wisdom. If you think about it, at that time, that was quite a risky endeavor for a number of the people involved. Actually, less risky in Scotland, which is one of the reasons why independent thinking flourished here. The second condition was tolerance, a willingness to hear other people voice ideas that we don't agree with. Again, at that time, you could be hanged for heresies. This spirit

185

of tolerance and convivial conversation that grew up in the coffee clubs and drinking clubs around Edinburgh and elsewhere at that time were an essential enabling condition for the conversation of ideas. The third one that he mentioned was the rootedness in practice. As he said, Adam Smith lived down Glasgow and he was down at the quay side every day talking to the merchants and the traders, and asking, "Well, what is the world like out there?" When Alexander Brody came here to talk about this, he said one of the reasons why St. Andrews University, although the oldest university in Scotland, played little part in the first enlightenment, was because it was so far off the beaten track. As he put it, St. Andrews was a bunch of academics looking into each other's graves.

Fortunately, we learned in retrospect, that we had started to recreate those three conditions--the independence of thought, the tolerance and the conviviality in the conversation, the rootedness in practice in our own practice. It was David Hume who said the truth is arrived at through argument between friends. We had both the argument and the friendship, even if a lot of arguments missed the friendship element, and we had the rootedness in practice. You must put your ideas into practice and you must derive your ideas from practice, from which one of our little prompt cards says redesign the plane whilst flying it, which captures that tight connection between theory and practice. These are some of the enabling conditions that actually are 250 years old. They worked at that time and they're working for us too.

Hodgson: I think in the spirit of nostalgia for the future, then we're perhaps coming to a kind of provisional conclusion here at this stage of our conversation, which is that we need to put policy aside in it's usual form, we need to put strategy aside in it's usual form, and we need to put design in the center. The next design revolution is to shift it from just the domain of the physical embodiment of good living, into the whole complex structure, including culture, governments, consciousness. The heart of the enterprise needs to be designing the future. If we don't design the future, I think many of us are aware of the kind of future we'll get, and that isn't the one that we want.

" WITHOUT THIS PLAYING OF FANTASY,
NO CREATIVE WORK HAS EVER YET COME
TO BIRTH...THE DEBT WE OWE TO THE PLAY
OF IMAGINATION IS INCALCULABLE."
Jung

City21/Index:

Acknowledgements:

The Editors hereby acknowledge the influence of the following people and places for their role in helping to shape the research and development that went into this book making endeavor:

-the late Ian McHarg for his mentorship and grand conception skills

-the late Marc Camporeale for his steadfast friendship over the years

-Phil Hawes for the audacity of his Vision

-Laurence Chassagne for her French aesthetics and abiding support

-Sunrock Farm for being the creative space in which to create

-The New Jersey towns of Mays Landing and Cape May for whoose hollow-ness help stimulate the quest for alternatives to the business as usual approach hat keeps too many American municipalities in the realm of languor.

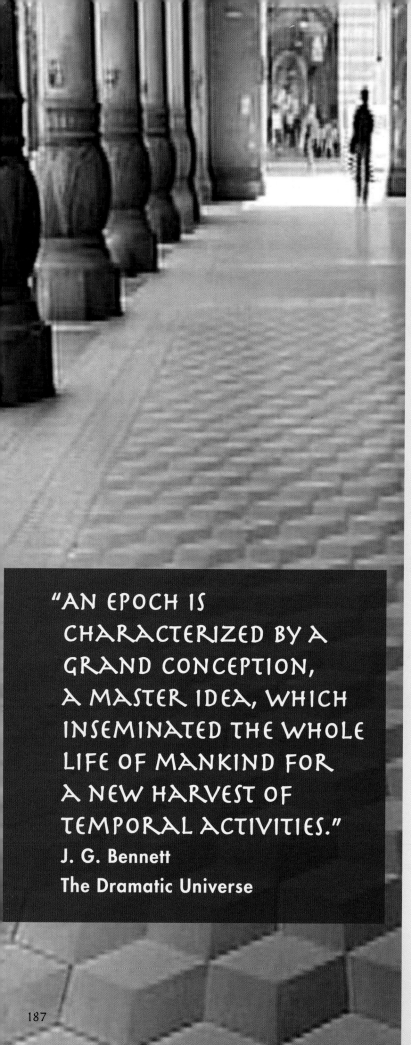

"AN EPOCH IS CHARACTERIZED BY A GRAND CONCEPTION, A MASTER IDEA, WHICH INSEMINATED THE WHOLE LIFE OF MANKIND FOR A NEW HARVEST OF TEMPORAL ACTIVITIES."
J. G. Bennett
The Dramatic Universe

What is a City?

1. **An Extension of the Village**

2. **A Matrix of Information**

3. **A Spatial Arrangement of People and Resources**

4. **A Political Configuration**

5. **A Traditional Way of Living**

6. **A Police Force**

7. **A Set of Laws to Live By**

8. **The Basis of Civilization**

9. **The Management of Water**

10. **A Mysterious Labyrinth**

11. **A Social System of Survival**

12. **A Place Where They Tow Cars**

13. **Microcosm of the Cosmos (Chinese City)**

14. **Occupied by People Who Have Left the Land**

15. **A Place Where Cafe's and Conversations Abound**

16. **A Place Where Civilization Began**

17. **A Holy Fire**
"Romulus Set-Up an Alter and Lighted a Fire Upon It. This Was the Holy Fire of the City."

The Ancient City ©2005
A School for Advanced Research
Resident Scholar Book

18. **A New Environment Created by an Ever Changing Cast of Characters**

19. **A Series of Concentric Zones Proceeding Outward from a Center**

20. **Diverse Sectors Crosscutting Concentric Rings**

21. **Energy and Communication forms evolving through time since the first urban settlement in ancient Sumer**

22. **A Net Exporter of Energy and Intelligence**

23. **A sacred place guarded by a Sphinx, who asks a riddle to travelers who seek to enter**

Bibliography

ALISON, JANE; BRAYER, MARIE-ANGE; MIGAYROU, FREDERIC; SPILLER, NEIL, Editors, Future City, London, UK: Barbican, 2006.

ALLEN, JOHN; NELSON, MARK, Space Biospheres, Oracle, AZ: Synergetic Press Inc., Second Edition 1989.

ANDERSON, WALTER TRUETT, Reality, San Francisco, CA: Harper & Row Publishers Inc., 1990.

ANTONIOU, JIM, Cities Then & Now, New York: MacMillan, 1994.

ARGAN, GIULIO C., The Renaissance City, New York: George Braziller Inc.,

1969.

ARTAUD, ANTONIN, The Theater and Its Double, New York: Grove Press Inc., 1958.

ASHTON, JOHN; WHYTE, TOM, The Quest for Paradise, San Francisco, CA: Harper & Row Publishers Inc., 2001.

BACON, EDMUND N., Design of Cities, New York: Penguin Books, Reprinted 1980.

BANG, JAN MARTIN, Ecovillages, Gabriola Island, Canada: New Society Publishers, 2005.

BECKER, CARL L., The Heavenly City of the Eighteenth-Century Philosophers, New Haven, CT: Yale University Press, Second Edition 2003.

BERGDOLL, BARRY; GAMBONI, DARIO; URSPRUNG, PHILIP, Essays: Nature Design, Baden, Switzerland: Lars Muller Publishers, 2007.

BERGER, ALAN, Drosscape, New York: Princeton Architectural Press, 2006.

BERRY, THOMAS, The Great Work, New York: Bell Tower, 1999.

   The Dream of the Earth, San Francisco, CA: Sierra Club Books, 1990.

BOGLIOLO, KARIN; NEWFELD, CARLY, Magic of Findhorn, Scotland, UK: Findhorn Press, 2002.

BORCHERT, JOHN R., Megalopolis, New Brunswick, NJ: Rutgers University Press, 1992.

BOULLEE; LEDOUX; LEQUEU, Visionary Architects, Santa Monica, CA: Hennessey+Ingalls, Reprinted 2002.

BRAND, STEWART, The Clock of The Long Now, New York: Basic Books, 1999.

BURDEN, ERNEST, Visionary Architecture, New York: McGraw-Hill Companies Inc., 2000.

BURKE, JAMES, The Knowledge Web, New York: Touchstone, 2000.

CAHILL, THOMAS, Mysteries of the Middle Ages, New York: First Anchor Books Edition, 2008.

CAMPBELL, JOSEPH, Creative Mythology, New York: Penguin Putnam Inc., Reprinted 1976.

CASSIRER, ERNST, The Philosophy of Symbolic Forms, New Haven, CT: Yale University Press, 1955.

CLARKE, DAVID B., Editor, The Cinematic City, New York: Routledge, Reprinted 2002.

COHAT, YVES, The Vikings: Lords of the Seas, New York: Harry N. Abrams Inc., 1992.

COOK, PETER, Editor, Archigram, New York: Princeton Architectural Press, 1999.

CORN, JOSEPH J.; HORRIGAN, BRIAN, Yesterday's Tomorrows, Baltimore, MD: The Johns Hopkins University Press, Reprinted 1996.

DAWSON, JONATHAN, Ecovillages, White River Junction, VT: Chelsea Green Publishing Company, 2006.

DELEVOY, ROBERT L., Symbolists and Symbolism, New York: Rizzoli International Publications Inc., Reprinted 1982.

DE MILLE, RICHARD, Castaneda's Journey, Lincoln, NE: iUniverse.com Inc., 2000.

DI FRANCESCO, CARLA; BORELLA, MARCO, Ferrara, Bologna, Italy: Italcards.

DOMOSH, MONA, Invented Cities, New Haven, CT: Yale University Press, 1996.

DOXIADIS, C. A., Anthropopolis, New York: Norton & Company Inc.

DUANY, ANDRES; PLATER-ZYBERK, ELIZABETH; SPECK, JEFF, Suburban Nation, New York: North Point Press, 2000.

EATON, RUTH, Ideal Cities, New York: Thames & Hudson Inc., 2001.

EISELEY, LOREN, The Lost Notebooks of Loren Eiseley, Lincoln, NE: Bison Books, University of Nebraska Press, 2002.

The Unexpected Universe, Orlando, FL: Harcourt Brace & Company, renewed 3rd 1994.

The Star Thrower, New York: Harcourt, 1978.

FIDELER, DAVID, Editor, Alexandria, Grand Rapids, MI: Phanes Press, 1993.

FOX, MATTHEW, Creativity, New York: Tarcher/Penguin, 2004.

GIRARDET, HERBERT, Creating Sustainable Cities, Devon, UK: The Schumacher Society, 1999
Cities, New York: Anchor Books, 1993.

GIROUARD, MARK, Cities & People, New Haven, CT: Yale University Press, Second Printing 1986.

GOLDWATER, ROBERT, Symbolism, New York: Harper & Row Publishers Inc., 1979.

GOODMAN, NELSON, Ways of Worldmaking, Indianapolis, IN: Hackett Publishing Company Inc., 1978.

GRAU, CHRISTOPHER, The Matrix, New York: Oxford University Press Inc., 2005.

HALL, PETER, Cities of Tomorrow, New York: Basil Blackwell Inc., Reprinted 1989.

HANCOCK, GRAHAM; BAUVAL, ROBERT, Talisman, London, UK: Element, Harper Collins Publishers, 2004.

HANNIGAN, JOHN, Fantasy City, New York: Routledge, 1998.

HARMAN, WILLIS W., Ph.D.; SAHTOURIS, ELISABET, Ph.D., Biology Revisioned, Berkeley, CA: North Atlantic Books, 1998.

HARMAN, WILLIS W., Ph.D.; RHEINGOLD, HOWARD, Higher Creativity, New York: Tarcher/Penguin, 1984.

HARTMANN, THOM, The Last Hours of Ancient Sunlight, New York: Three Rivers Press, Revised and Updated 2004.

HILBERSEIMER, L., The Nature of Cities, Chicago, Il: Paul Theobald Company, 1955.

HUIZINGA, JOHAN, Homo Ludens, Boston, MA: The Beacon Press, 1955.

HUSSERL, EDMUND, The Idea of Phenomenology, The Hague, Netherlands: Martinus Nijhoff, 1964.

JACOBS, JANE, The Death and Life of Great American Cities, New York: Vintage Books Edition, 1992.

JAEGER, WERNER, Paideia, New York: Oxford University Press, second Printing 1967.

JENCKS, CHARLES, Architecture 2000, New York: Praeger Publishers Inc., 1971.

JENKS, MIKE; DEMPSEY, NICOLA, Future Forms and Design for Sustainable Cities, Burlington, MA: Architectural Press, 2005.

KIRK, ANDREW G., Counterculture Green, Lawrence, KS: University Press of Kansas, 2007.

KOTKIN, JOEL, The City, New York: Modern Library Edition, 2005.

KORTEN, DAVID C., The Great Turning, San Francisco, CA: Berrett-Koehler Publishers Inc.; Bloomfield, CT: Kumarian Press Inc., 2006.

KOSTOF, SPIRO, America by Design, New York: Oxford University Press Inc., 1987.

The City Assembled, London, UK: Thames & Hudson Ltd., 1992.

KUNSTLER, JAMES HOWARD, The City in Mind, New York: The Free Press, 2001.

LANDRY, CHARLES, The Art of City Making, Sterling, VA: Earthscan, 2006.

The Creative City, Sterling, VA: Earthscan, Reprinted 2002.

LERUP, LARS, After the City, Cambridge, MA: The M.I.T. Press, 2001.

LETHABY, W. R., Architecture, Mysticism and Myth, New York: Cosimo Inc., Reprinted 2005.

LIETAER, BERNARD, The Future of Money, London, UK: Century, 2001.

LORIE, PETER; MURRAY-CLARK, SIDD, History of the Future, New York: Doubleday, 1989.

LOVELOCK, JAMES, The Ages of Gaia , New York: Norton & Company Inc., 1988.

LYNCH, KEVIN, The Image of the City, First M.I.T. Press Paperback Edition, Fifth Printing 1968.

McNALLY, MARCIA, Blueprint for a Sustainable Bay Area, San Francisco, CA: Urban Ecology Inc., 1996.

MARRAS, AMERIGO, Editor, Eco-Tec Architecture of the In-Between, New York: Princeton Architectural Press, 1999.

MARSHALL, ALEX, How Cities Work, Austin, TX: University of Texas Press, Fifth Printing 2003.

MARTINES, LAURO, Power and Imagination, New York: Alfred A. Knopf Inc.,1979.

MATANOVIC, MILENKO, Meandering Rivers and Square Tomatoes, Issaquah, WA: Morningtown Press, 1988.

MAYERNIK, DAVID, Timeless Cities, Boulder, CO: Westview Press, 2003.

MEYROWITZ, JOSHUA, No Sense of Place, New York: Oxford University Press, 1985.

MITCHELL, WILLIAM J., E-topia, Cambridge, MA: The M.I.T. Press, 1999.

MORE, THOMAS, Utopia, London, UK: Penguin Books, 2003.

MOUGHTIN, CLIFF, Urban Design, Oxford, UK: Butterworth Architecture, 1996.

MUMFORD, LEWIS, The City in History, New York: Harcourt, Brace & World Inc., 1961.

The Highway and The City, New York: Mentor Book, 1964.

Architecture as a Home for Man, New York: Architectural Record Books, 1975.

O'GORMAN, EDMUNDO, The Invention of America, Bloomington, IN: Indiana University Press, 1961.

NICHOLS, BILL, Representing Reality, Bloomington, IN: Indiana University Press, 1991.

NEUSTADT, RICHARD E.; MAY, ERNEST R., Thinking in Time, New York: The Free Press, 1988.

ORR, DAVID W., The Nature of Design, New York: Oxford University Press Inc., 2002.

PALMER, MARTIN; PALMER, NIGEL, Sacred Britain, London, UK: Judy Piatkus Ltd, Reprinted 1999.

PANOFSKY, ERWIN, Perspective as Symbolic Form, New York: Urzone Inc., Third Printing 2002.

PARSONS, KERMIT C.; SCHUYLER, DAVID, Editors, From Garden City to Green City, Baltimore, MD: The Johns Hopkins University Press, 2002.

PAZ, OCTAVIO, Essays: Convergences, Orlando, FL: Harcourt Brace Jovanovich Inc., 1987.

PENDLETON-JULLIAN, ANN M., The Road that is Not a Road, Cambridge, MA: The M.I.T. Press, 1996.

PEVSNER, NIKOLAUS, The Sources of Modern Architecture and Design, New York: Thames & Hudson Inc., Reprinted 2004.

POLAK, FRED. L., The Image of the Future, New York: Sythoff Oceana, 1961.

RAINE, KATHLEEN, William Blake, New York: Thames and Hudson Inc., Reprinted 1996. Golgonooza, Hudson, NY: Lindisfarne Press, 1991.

REGISTER, RICHARD; PEEKS, BRADY, Editors, Village Wisdom / Future Cities, Oakland, CA: Ecocity Builders, 1997.

RIEMEN, ROB, Nobility of Spirit, New Haven, CT: Yale University Press, 2008.

ROSELAND, MARK, Editor, Eco-City, New Haven, CT: New Society Publishers, 1997.

RYKWERT, JOSEPH, The Idea of a Town, Princeton, NJ: Princeton University Press, Second Printing 1989.

The Seduction of Place, New York: Vintage Books, 2002.

SAARINEN, ELIEL, The City, New York: Reinhold Publishing Corporation, Fourth Printing 1958.

SADLER, SIMON, The Situationist City, Cambridge, MA: The M.I.T. Press, 1998.

SAINT AUGUSTINE, City of God, New York: Doubleday, 1958.

SCHAER, ROLAND; CLAEYS, GREGORY; TOWER SARGENT, LYMAN, Utopia, New York: The New York Public Library, 2000.

SCHIFFER, ROBERT L., The Exploding City, New York: St. Martin's Press, 1989.

SCHNEIDER, MICHAEL S., Constructing the Universe, New York: First Harper Perennial, Reprinted 1995.

SCHONING, PASCAL, Manifesto for a Cinematic Architecture, London, UK: Architectural Association Publications, 2006.

SCHWARTZ, PETER, The Art of the Long View, New York: Currency Doubleday, 1996.

SITTE, CAMILLO, The Birth of Modern City Planning, Mineola, NY: Dover Publications Inc.,

Reprinted 2006.

SOLERI, PAOLO, Technology and Cosmogenesis, New York: Paragon House Publishers, Reprinted 1985.

SPAID, SUE, Ecovention, Cincinnati, OH: The Contemporary Arts Center, 2002.

SPANGLER, DAVID; THOMPSON, WILLIAM IRWIN, Reimagination of the World, Santa Fe, NM: Bear&Company Inc., 1991.

SPILLER, NEIL, Visionary Architecture, New York: Thames & Hudson, 2007.

SPINOSA, CHARLES; FLORES, FERNANDO; DREYFUS, HUBERT L., Disclosing New Worlds, Cambrige, MA: The M.I.T. Press, 1997.

TINNISWOOD, ADRIAN, Visions of Power, New York: Stewart, Tabori, Chang, 1998.

THOMPSON, WILLIAM IRWIN, Self and Society, Charlottesville, VA: Imprint Academic, 2004. Transforming History, Great Barrington, MA: Lindisfarne Books, 2001.

TODD, JOHN; TODD, NANCY JACK, The Village as Solar Ecology, East Falmouth, MA: The New Alchemy Institute, 1980.

TSCHUMI, BERNARD, Event-Cities 2, Cambridge, MA: The M.I.T. Press, 2000.

VAN DER RYN, SIM, Design for Life, Layton, UT: Gibbs Smith, 2005.

VERNADSKY, VLADIMIR I., The Biosphere, New York: Copernicus, 1998.

WALLACE-MURPHY, TIM, Cracking the Symbol Code, London, UK: Watkins

WEISMAN, ALAN, Gaviotas, White River Junction, VT: Chelsea Green Publishing Company, 1998.

WINES, JAMES, Green Architecture, Koln, Germany: Taschen, 2000.

WOLF, PETER, The Future of the City, New York: Whitney Library of Design, 1974.

WRIGHT, FRANK LLOYD, The Living City, New York: Bramhall House, 1958.

YATES, FRANCES A., The Art of Memory, London,UK: Pimlico, 2005.

compiled by Laurence Chassagne

WHO WILLS THE ENDS, WILL THE MEANS

"The rise and fall of images of the future preceeds or accompanies the rise and fall of cultures. As long as society's image is positive and flourishing, the flower of culture is in full blook. Once the image begins to decay and lose its vitality, however the culture does not long survive."

Fred Polak

This book is part of an ongoing quest for insight into creating the future of the City.

To find out more, and to participate, visit the website: www.city21.info

To discover more about **The Knossus Project** visit: www.geniusloci.com

CASTILLON

CONTRIBUTOR BIOGRAPHIES:

Stewart Brand is an American writer, editor, and futurist. He founded the Whole Earth Catalog, The Well, the Global Business Network and the Long Now Foundation. His many books include: The Clock of the Long Now, How Buildings Learn, and Whole Earth Discipli

Jonathan Dawson is a sustainability educator and President of the Global Eco-village Network, who is based at the Findhorn Foundation in Scotland.

Craig Gibsone is a long term member of Findhorn and is Manager of the Findhorn Studios which featured the famed Pottery, Weaving, Printing, and Candle Making studios.

Yvonne Cunco is a member of the Communications Team and Foundation Management Tec Findhorn.

Loren Eiseley was an American anthropologist, educator, philosopher, poet, and natural science writer. Eiseley received thirty-six honorary degrees, was provost at the University o Pennsylvania, and the author of many books including the classics The Immense Journey, Darwin's Century, and The Lost Notebooks.

Falco (Oberto Airaudi) is a philosopher, painter, writer, healer, and founder and spiritual of the Foundation of Damanhur, the experimental, esoteric community, often described as Eighth Wonder of the World, located near Turin, Italy.

Esperides Ananas is the Communications Director of Damanhur, and a key contributor to Damanhur: Temples of Mankind.

Graham Leicester is the Director of International Futures Forum and former member of HM Diplomatic Service, whose focus and expertise is in governance, innovation, education, an the arts.

Paolo Lugari has been described by Gabriel Garcia Marquez as the "inventor of the worl for his work as the founder, in 1971, and director of the ecovillage of Gaviotas, Columbia.

David Mayernik is a practicing urban designer, architect, artist, professor of architecture a Notre Dame University, and author of Timeless Cities: An Architect's Reflections on Renaissance Italy.

Lori McElroy is and environmental engineer and directs the SUST project on sustainability for the Policy Unit, at The Lighthouse, in Glasgow, Scotland.

Phil Hawes is an architect, town and regional designer who specializes in sustainable community development and Eco-Village design. He was the architect-of-record of Biosphere 2, in Oracle, Arizona., and is currently the president of Ecological Systems Design.

Tony Hodgson is the founder of Decision Integrity Limited, a company pioneering ways to holistic thinking, systems mapping, integrative group processes and sustainable values. He is a founding member of the International Futures Forum and contributing member of the Oxford Futures Forum.

David Jolly is an active member of the Open City Group, and a Chilean architect.

Juan Purcell is a Chilean architect and one of the founders of the Valparaiso School, based at the Open City, a utopian community in Ritoque, Chile.

Adalsteinn Sigurgeirsson is the head of Iceland Forest Research, near Reykjavik, and vice-chairman of the Reykjavik Forestation Association.

Arnold J. Toynbee was a British philosopher and self-described "meta-historian" whose major work was the controversial twelve-volume A Study in History, which chronicled the rise and fall of world civilizations.

So here ends **City21: The Search for the 2nd Enlightenment**. On this day the 4th of July 2010, Christopher Zelov, Phil Cousineau, and William J. Cohen have completed version 1.0 of this epic quest.

VIVENDO DESCIMUS

The fonts used in this production include: Crofter, Baskerville, Classic Scotland, Futura.